Praise for *The College Solut*

"Do yourself a favor and read this book when your child is a sophomore. You'll save money and forgo big headaches."

—Richard Lee Colvin, Director, Hechinger Institute on Education and the Media, Teachers College, Columbia University

"Worried about how you're going to pay for a great college education? Read Lynn O'Shaughnessy's book to find some surprising answers!"

—Rick Darvis, CPA, Founder, National Institute of Certified College Planners

"The beauty of higher education in the U.S. is its range of possibilities—from our accessible community college system to our public colleges and research universities and the private options topped by the highly selective Ivy League. Lynn O'Shaughnessy evaluates the array of choices available to prospective students and guides families through the search and selection process. She has done a fine job of demystifying what can be an emotional journey."

—Kathleen Teehan, Vice Chancellor for Enrollment Management, University of Massachusetts, Boston

"In clear, easy-to-understand language, Lynn O'Shaughnessy explains how choosing the right colleges to apply to in the first place can not only ultimately improve a student's chances of admission, but their family's ability to pay the tab."

—Carolyn Z. Lawrence, Creator, AdmissionsAdvice.com

"*The College Solution* offers a refreshing and remarkably user-friendly approach to the otherwise menacing college application process. A lucid and exceptionally practical work, *The College Solution* focuses on strategies for parents and students alike as they navigate the increasingly arduous journey to discover the right school at the right price."

—Brett Peterson, Director, High Tech High, San Diego

"*The College Solution* provides a realistic approach to so many family concerns regarding a college plan."

—Herman Davis, Ed.D, College Financial Aid for Dummies

"I congratulate Lynn O'Shaughnessy for making a significant contribution to the college planning process of finding the best match. She takes a process that can be quite overwhelming and offers practical, action-oriented steps that will provide clarity and a greater sense of control. The book is rich with resources and exceptionally clear and well-organized. I highly recommend it to families anticipating or already in the midst of applying to colleges."

—Timothy B. Lee, President, Independent Educational Consultants Association (IECA)

"*The College Solution* offers a no-nonsense, common sense approach to exploring colleges—challenging students to dig deeper when researching schools to reveal the unique academic differences between institutions. Sadly, this in-depth investigation by students is often missing. Lynn does a wonderful job of providing students with alternative sources to use when collecting information about a college. The tips provided on how to best utilize a college's website and other outside sources (such as emailing professors directly) is right on target."

—Lisa R. Micele, Director of College Counseling, University of Illinois Laboratory High School, Urbana, Illinois

"I encourage current and future college students and their parents to read this book. Forewarned is forearmed!"

—Alan M. Collinge, StudentLoanJustice.org

"While price should never be the first consideration because of aid possibilities, this book does a great job of explaining the ins and outs of financing the right "fit" for students. A must read for any college-bound high school student and parents. Lynn O'Shaughnessy has done a masterful job!"

—Dr. Robert Massa, Vice President for Enrollment and College Relations, Dickinson College, Carlisle, Pennsylvania

"O'Shaughnessy's comprehensive, common-sense book is a must-read for students and families beginning the college search process, especially because she highlights scores of lesser-known colleges across the country that 'provide an education as good as or superior to' that offered by many better known colleges. She also correctly notes that, thanks to generous financial aid packages, many private liberal arts colleges are as affordable as the state universities."

—Richard Ekman, President, Council of Independent Colleges, Washington D.C.

"Savvy, supportive, and sensible, *The College Solution* offers a wealth of candid and practical advice about college choice and the true reality of financing one's higher education. The author invites parents and students to get beyond the usual suspects when seeking out schools, debunks the myths of selectivity and wanton expensiveness masquerading as academic superiority, and offers a refreshingly straightforward approach to college choice."

—Dan Golden, Director of Life Planning and Experiential Learning, Vistamar School, El Segundo, California

"*The College Solution* provides parents and students with the tools they need to begin their understanding of what matters today in college admissions, encouragement to look beyond the name brands into what really makes for quality educational environments, and a sense of how they can afford to attend a mix of public and private colleges and universities."

—Matthew W. Greene, Ph.D, Howard Green and Associates, Westport, Connecticut

"Lynn O'Shaughnessy has done a masterful job in explaining many of the nuances of applying to college. The book delves into the rankings myth and encourages students and parents to look beyond the high name recognition schools. The book should be a resource for students and parents in the high school years."

—Leslie Chase, College Resource Teacher, Pine View School, Osprey, Florida

"Lynn O'Shaughnessy provides sanity in the midst of a process gone mad."

—Deborah Hirsch, Ed.D., Associate Vice President for Academic Affairs, Mount Ida College, Newton, Massachusetts

"Finally, the first comprehensive guide to overcoming the mysteries of financial aid and the college search process! Through a well researched effort, O'Shaughnessy has created an indispensable guide for every family willing to spend the time required to prepare for a wonderfully successful college search. There is nothing else like it on the market and families and especially future college students will really benefit by finding the right college at a reasonably affordable price."

—Thomas Kepple, President, Juniata College, Huntingdon, Pennsylvania

"Lynn O'Shaughnessy has written the book that every parent needs to read before sending a child off to college. Her strategies can help the next generation of scholars get outstanding, affordable educations without mortgaging their futures to debt."

—Liz Pulliam Weston, Personal Finance Columnist, MSN Money

"For students and parents who are desperate for good, common sense information and advice about college admissions, *The College Solution* is just what the doctor ordered. The guide is particularly useful for people wanting sound direction about financial aid, something that most other admissions books don't cover. You need to have Lynn O'Shaughnessy's sage advice as early as sophomore year."

—Marjorie Hansen Shaevitz, Director, adMISSIONPOSSIBLE.com, La Jolla, California

"BRAVO! A no-nonsense, easy-to-read guide that skillfully weaves together the synergy between the admission and financial aid processes. Don't wait until the junior year of high school to read this book."

—Marguerite J. Dennis, Vice President Enrollment and International Programs, Suffolk University, Boston

"Concise information, valuable resources, and honest guidance are the cornerstones for every parent looking to help their child get into and pay for college, and Lynn O'Shaughnessy has provided just that in *The College Solution*."

—John P. Derham, Chief Marketing Officer, MyRichUncle Student Loans

the **COLLEGE** SOLUTION

the **COLLEGE** SOLUTION

A Guide for Everyone Looking for the Right School at the Right Price

Lynn O'Shaughnessy

Vice President, Publisher: Tim Moore
Associate Publisher and Director of Marketing: Amy Neidlinger
Executive Editor: Jim Boyd
Editorial Assistant: Heather Luciano
Development Editor: Russ Hall
Operations Manager: Gina Kanouse
Digital Marketing Manager: Julie Phifer
Publicity Manager: Laura Czaja
Assistant Marketing Manager: Megan Colvin
Marketing Assistant: Brandon Smith
Cover Designer: John Barnett
Managing Editor: Kristy Hart
Project Editor: Chelsey Marti
Copy Editor: Geneil Breeze
Proofreader: Kathy Ruiz
Senior Indexer: Cheryl Lenser
Compositor: Jake McFarland
Manufacturing Buyer: Dan Uhrig

Publishing as FT Press
Upper Saddle River, New Jersey 07458

FT Press offers excellent discounts on this book when ordered in quantity for bulk purchases or special sales. For more information, please contact U.S. Corporate and Government Sales, 1-800-382-3419, corpsales@pearsontechgroup.com. For sales outside the U.S., please contact International Sales at international@pearson.com.

Printed in the United States of America

Second Printing: August 2008
ISBN-10: 0-132-36570-7
ISBN-13: 978-0-13-236570-3

Pearson Education LTD.
Pearson Education Australia PTY, Limited
Pearson Education Singapore, Pte. Ltd.
Pearson Education North Asia, Ltd.
Pearson Education Canada, Ltd.
Pearson Educatiốn de Mexico, S.A. de C.V.
Pearson Education—Japan
Pearson Education Malaysia, Pte. Ltd.

Library of Congress Cataloging-in-Publication Data

O'Shaughnessy, Lynn, 1955-

The college solution : a guide for everyone looking for the right school at the right price / Lynn O'Shaughnessy.

p. cm.

ISBN 0-13-236570-7 (pbk. : alk. paper) 1. College student orientation—United States. 2. College choice—United States. 3. Student aid—United States. I. Title.

LB2343.32.O82 2008

378.73—dc22

2008005626

To Ben, Caitlin, and Bruce

Contents

Acknowledgments

When my parents contemplated sending their five children to college, they concluded that my mother would have to start teaching again to help pay the education bills. My parents had always been frugal—I don't recall eating a single steak growing up—but frugality couldn't cover what they faced: 20 years of college costs.

Because my mother, who had left the teaching profession when her oldest child was born, headed back to the classroom, my parents managed to cover the college expenses of their kids. They watched all five of us graduate from the University of Missouri without going into debt.

At the time, I didn't dwell on my parents' amazing accomplishment, but as I fretted about how my husband and I were going to pay the college costs for our son and daughter, I marveled at their feat. I also realized that with today's runaway costs, simply having two parents chipping away at the college tab could still leave families seriously in debt.

Consequently, I set out on a mission to see how we could afford wonderful colleges for our teenagers at the most affordable prices. I've been a financial journalist for many years, so it has always been easy for me to write about such topics as retirement accounts, mutual funds, and investing. But discovering winning college strategies required considerable effort because remarkably this is an area that few people—outside the higher education community—really know much about.

In getting acclimated to this new field, I began reading *The Chronicle of Higher Education* and the online industry publication *Inside Higher Ed*. I also interviewed top education experts as I conducted research while writing stories for *Money* magazine, *BusinessWeek*, and publications from *Kiplinger's*, *Consumer Reports*, and AARP, as well as my own weekly syndicated financial column.

As I researched, I discovered some amazing organizations that provided me with a great education. They include the

HigherEdWatch.org blog of the New America Foundation, the Project on Student Debt, the Education Sector, *The Journal of Blacks in Higher Education*, the Center of Inquiry in the Liberal Arts at Wabash College, the National Survey of Student Engagement, Community College Survey of Student Engagement, the Teagle Foundation, and the Education Conservancy.

Among the experts I want to thank are Deborah Fox, a college financial expert in San Diego, who set me off on the right path. I am also indebted to Alan Collinge, the creator of StudentLoanJustice.org, and Mark Kantrowitz, the founder of FinAid.org, whose knowledge about college financing is truly encyclopedic. Rick Darvis, CPA, the founder of the National Institute of Certified College Planners, always found time to answer my questions—even when he was exercising on his treadmill. I also want to thank the staff of the Jack Kent Cooke Foundation, which shared its wisdom on community colleges, and George Kuh, the founder of the National Survey of Student Engagement, the Chancellor's Professor of Higher Education, and Director of the Center for Postsecondary Research at Indiana University School of Education.

I'm also grateful to Robert J. Massa, vice president for enrollment and college relations at Dickinson College, for his wise insight, as well as Martha "Marty" O'Connell, executive director of the Colleges That Change Lives organization, who shared her thoughts on the virtues of liberal arts colleges. And I was delighted to learn that one of my absolute favorite experts, Carolyn Z. Lawrence, creator of Admissions-Advice.com, lives just a few miles from me in San Diego County.

The College Solution would have never materialized had it not been for my editor, Jim Boyd, who possessed the foresight to realize that this book could be a lifesaver for any family with college-bound teenagers. I also appreciate the efforts of Geneil Breeze and Chelsey Marti to fine-tune the book's content.

Finally, I want to thank my husband, Bruce V. Bigelow, and our children, Caitlin and Ben, who experienced my mercurial author moods, as well as the breakdown of my aging iMac just days before my deadline. And I can't forget Minerva, our golden retriever, who kept me company through every line of this book.

About the Author

Lynn O'Shaughnessy has been a professional journalist for three decades. She is a former *Los Angeles Times* reporter and syndicated columnist, and a financial journalist. Her previous books include *Unofficial Guide to Investing, Investing Bible*, and *Retirement Bible*. She has contributed to such publications as *BusinessWeek*, *Money Magazine*, *USA Today*, *Chronicle of Philanthropy*, *AARP The Magazine*, *Wealth Manager Magazine*, *The New York Times*, *The Wall Street Journal, Kiplinger's Retirement Report*, *Bottom Line Personal*, and *Consumer Reports MoneyAdviser*. She is a graduate of the School of Journalism at the University of Missouri in Columbia.

Foreword

A few weeks ago, I had to break a student's heart by giving her some bad news. This particular student had worked hard throughout high school, earning solid grades while taking a full slate of challenging college prep courses.

She had participated in an impressive list of extracurricular activities, and spent many diligent hours preparing for her college entrance exams. Throughout her junior and senior years, she and her single mother had visited many college campuses, and she'd applied to a nice list of colleges. She'd ended up doing well in terms of admissions, getting accepted to five out of the six great colleges she'd applied to.

One particular college on her "accepted" list was her clear favorite. She'd been pleasantly surprised to be admitted to that college because her grades and test scores were a bit below the school's average. But, she had been admitted, and now she and her mother were sitting in my college counseling office with her financial aid award letter.

"They gave her a $10,000 scholarship!" the mother said excitedly. "We didn't expect that, and they're the only college that gave her a scholarship." The college had also included a $12,000 a year need-based institutional grant, $2,500 a year in federal work study, and a $3,500 annual federal loan.

That's when the bad news started to kick in. The cost of attending the student's dream college the following year would be just over $48,000, leaving a $28,000 gap between the college's price tag and the financial aid award.

The mother had the option of closing the gap through a Federal PLUS Loan for parents. That would have meant monthly payments of $223 a month spread out over the next ten years. But that would have only gotten her daughter through the first year. To pay for four years of college, the mother would have likely had to borrow at least $72,000, which would have generated monthly payments of $829.

What's more, the mother would still need to come up with $10,000 a year that the federal aid formula had determined was her fair share of her daughter's college expenses. "That'll be like having a second mortgage!" the mother said, as her daughter's face fell in disappointment.

My student and her mother aren't alone. Unfortunately, I've heard similar shock expressed time and time again by the families I work with as a college counselor, and seen the same look of disappointment on the faces of many students as they realize their "dream college" isn't in the works financially.

While popular media has loudly touted the increased competition for admissions to our nation's top colleges, the truth is, for many students, getting in isn't the problem. It's how to pay for college once you do get in.

Parents and students are having to make tough choices these days, and that's adding to an already stressful process. According to a recent poll conducted by *The New York Times* and CBS News, 70% of parents surveyed were "very concerned" about how they would pay for college. Only 6% of parents reported that they were not concerned with college costs.

As a financial journalist and parent of teenagers herself, Lynn O'Shaughnessy is uniquely qualified to tackle some of the tough choices families face as they look at college options for their children. She's started the discussion at exactly the right place: with the money side of the equation.

By providing a thorough overview of the many factors affecting college costs and financial aid today, and suggesting realistic solutions for solving the college cost crisis faced by most families, she gives both parents and students a blueprint for a realistic college search.

In clear, easy-to-understand language, she explains how choosing the right colleges to apply to in the first place can not only ultimately improve a student's chances of admission, but their family's ability to pay the tab. *The College Solution* is a wonderful resource for parents, whether their children are about to apply to college or are still many years away from high school.

Take its message to heart, and you'll lessen the likelihood of having to break disappointing news to your own child about the affordability of their "dream college."

Carolyn Z. Lawrence
Independent College Advisor
AdmissionsAdvice.com
Jamul, California

Introduction

A curious story appeared in *The New York Times* one day about the university that's the academic equivalent of the Yankees. The article captured the concerns of faculty, who worry that the teaching taking place at Harvard University isn't meeting the school's own vaunted standards. In fact, a professor lamented that some undergraduates, after spending four years at Harvard, don't know a single faculty member well enough to ask for a letter of recommendation.

Hmmm.

One student, who was interviewed, suggested that undergraduates ought to know that professors are too focused on research to put much effort into what happens in the classroom.

"You'd be stupid if you came to Harvard for the teaching," a Harvard senior and a Rhodes scholar told the *Times* reporter. "You go to a liberal arts college for teaching. You come to Harvard to be around some of the greatest minds on earth."

And he had more to say: "I think many people (at Harvard) spend a great deal of their time in large lecture classes, have little direct contact with professors, and are frustrated by poorly trained teaching fellows."

Concerned about the quality of Harvard's undergraduate education, a small group of the university's professors cranked out a report that advocated for institutional changes that would place greater value on teaching. Whatever happens, Harvard's institutional angst about what occurs in its classrooms is hardly going to dampen its star power among high school students. And that was true even before Harvard unveiled an incredibly generous financial aid policy that has dramatically cut costs for families who make even $180,000 per year.

So why have I begun this book by sharing something that should embarrass Harvard? Because the incident aptly illustrates one of the primary reasons why I wrote *The College Solution: A Guide for Everyone Looking for the Right School at the Right Price*. When many families begin their college search they assume that the Ivy League owns a monopoly on the nation's best schools. Unfortunately, the media perpetuates this nonsense. A ridiculous number of books on college are dedicated to cracking the Ivy League even though the only ivy that most kids are going to come into contact with will itch and require calamine lotion. A mere .2% of the nation's incoming college freshmen end up at the eight Ivy League schools.

What plenty of teenagers and their parents don't realize is that there are many, many schools scattered across the country that will provide an education as good as or superior to the one they'd receive at the most elite East Coast schools.

Rather than worship at the Ivy altar, *The College Solution* is dedicated to the 99.8% of students, who head off to the thousands of other colleges and universities in this country. It's about time that a book is dedicated to everybody else's kids—and there are millions of them out there. The book contains advice for teenagers who are blessed with the brilliance of theoretical physicist Stephen Hawking as well as all the typical kids who would fit in quite nicely at Lake Wobegon.

One of the book's overriding aims for this eclectic group of teenagers is this: helping them find the best academic matches possible, whether public or private, for the least amount of money. Parents and students, who use the book's road map, will discover that college costs can be far lower than they imagined and their college options are more plentiful than they ever would have believed.

Many families, for instance, assume that they can afford only an inexpensive school—perhaps the state university or community college that's nearby. The affluent, meanwhile, assume that they will have to pay full price for their children's education because their chances for any kind of assistance are laughable. Plenty of families, regardless of their net worth, believe that only the very brilliant or the athletically gifted can win scholarships.

All of those assumptions are wrong. College can be more affordable than you might think. "B" students can earn merit scholarships from plenty of colleges, and even families with six-figure incomes can position themselves to capture financial aid.

In fact, many families who use the book's strategies will be able to send their children off to expensive private schools for the same cost of a much cheaper in-state public school. Private colleges and universities today, according to the College Board, are discounting their tuition by an average of 33.5% for the students they want. Students who attend public universities, including prestigious flagship institutions, can also pay significantly less than the advertised sticker price. The average tuition discount for public schools, which cost less to begin with, is nearly 15%.

It's much easier to shrink the college tab once you appreciate that colleges and universities are now pricing bachelor's degrees in much the same way that airlines set their ticket prices. The passenger sitting next to you on the plane could have paid significantly more or less than you did for the identical ride. This same phenomenon is playing out on college and university campuses throughout the country.

The College Solution also urges parents and students to consider what is important in a college education. One of the chief aims of the book is to help students determine which schools are best for them and to encourage them to consider some overlooked academic gems. The book shows teenagers how to evaluate schools from research universities and community colleges to public and private liberal arts colleges.

Investigating schools, as you'll learn, should go far beyond noting what ranking a school got from *U.S. News & World Report*, which happens to rely on dubious methodology. When selecting schools, a student also needs to be comfortable with the academic departments where he or she will be spending a great deal of time. You want professors who will engage students with innovative teaching, not approach classes, particularly the introductory ones, as an opportunity to wash out kids by dispensing failing grades. You'll also discover how to find large universities that have worked hard to make their learning environments more intimate.

Most students will have only one shot at college, but too often they put about as much effort into finding the right academic matches as they would shopping for a new cell phone plan. Families often take shortcuts because they swallow the conventional wisdom that the higher education industry has pushed down their throats about what their options are. Your best defense against all this is to keep reading this book.

Part I

Capturing Financial Aid

1

Where Is the $$$?

Colleges have gotten increasingly good at price discriminating. The list price is set high, and then many customers are offered a discount called "financial aid" based on their ability to pay. Here's the secret plan: In the future, Harvard will cost $1 billion a year, and only Bill Gates's children will pay full price. When anyone else walks through the door, the message will be "Special price, just for you."

—Greg Mankiw, professor of economics at Harvard University

When you're visiting colleges, the campus tour guides understand that certain areas are off limits. They aren't going to have you traipse through the cafeteria kitchen where the discarded pizza crusts mix with soap suds, and you won't be trolling past the financial aid administrators' cubicles.

Why disturb a family's wonderment at the beauty of the campus and perhaps the school's great perch in the *U.S. News & World Report* rankings with such prosaic concerns as how much this is going to cost—much less where the money is going to come from?

But before your child heads off to college, you will probably end up getting acquainted with the financial aid staffers who will be bundling together potential financial aid packages for your child. By the time the process is complete, these paper shufflers could know more about your finances than perhaps anyone else on earth, even more than the Internal Revenue Service does.

While colleges are entitled to learn the most intimate details of families' financial lives, most parents are clearly at a disadvantage in this process. That's because they typically harbor no clue about how colleges make decisions. And if your strategy is to depend on the kindness of a college administrator, you could very well be disappointed.

Mastering how financial aid is dispensed—or at least knowing enough to benefit your own family—will probably seem about as appealing as reading a digital camera's instruction manual. But understanding the basics is essential because the costs, especially for private schools, can be staggering. Colleges don't face the same predicament as McDonald's or KFC, which must agonize over the potential of losing customers if they boost the price of a Big Mac or bucket of chicken. Even Starbucks, which has so many of us addicted to lattes and frappuccinos, has to be careful about raising its prices too high for fear of turning caffeine lovers into tea drinkers.

Colleges, however, have not been punished for raising their prices far beyond the rate of inflation each year. In fact, as perverse as this may seem, some schools have jacked up their prices to attract affluent families who assume that if the cost isn't exorbitant, the school must not be any good.

Colleges have been sitting in a supply-and-demand sweet spot. Since the early 1990s, applications from high school seniors continued to rise as the Baby Boomers' children entered college. The number of high school graduates, however, peaked in 2008 when roughly 3.34 million earned a diploma. More than 60% of those kids will be heading to college. In contrast, the last time there was such a surge in applicants—in the mid 1970s when the Baby Boomers were in their teens and early twenties—less than half of high school graduates even bothered with college.

Even after high school graduation rates have peaked, the number of teenagers heading to college is expected to continue to grow as more of them decide that a college education is essential. The difference in lifetime earning power between a student who stops with a high school education and someone who earns a bachelor's degree is roughly $1.2 million. The financial advantage between someone who obtains a professional degree, such as a law degree, versus those who are satisfied with a bachelor's degree is an additional $1.7 million.

Thanks to the high price of a college degree today, two-thirds of all families receive some sort of financial aid. But as you'll learn, some types of aid are infinitely better than others. Grants, which don't need to be repaid, are going to be far more welcome than a federally guaranteed loan or work study. Not too long ago, 60% of the typical college's financial aid award was packaged with free cash. Loans represented the other 40%. But today, those numbers have been reversed. Loans now make up 60% of the average package.

Follow the Money Trail

You will increase your chances of obtaining a financial aid package that is fair or even more than fair if you understand how the process works. The families who get the most financial aid aren't always the ones who need it the most. Those who educate themselves will increase their chances of walking away with a package they can celebrate. But before you can do that, you'll need to understand the basics that you'll find in the next eight chapters.

Action Plan

If you educate yourself on your financial and academic choices, you are far more likely to slash the cost of college.

2

Looking for Cash in the Right Places

Higher education in America is big business. The college is trying to get you to pay the most money; you are trying to pay the least amount. It can be very costly to assume that the college is going to show you how to get the most aid. As a college financial aid administrator quoted in The New York Times *once said, "Parents and students sometimes forget that we work for the school, not for them."*

—Kalman A. Chany, president of Campus Consultants Inc. and author of *Paying For College Without Going Broke*

When teenagers begin looking for schools, the price is often not something they think much about. That's why I wasn't surprised when a mom told me about the experience of her daughter's boyfriend, who was thrilled to get an acceptance letter from the University of Notre Dame.

The boy, who was a phenomenal student, was shocked at how little money Notre Dame gave him to defray the cost. The future journalism major was even more worried because his parents weren't going to provide much financial help. He now assumes he will have to juggle multiple campus jobs with a tough course load.

Although money was a real issue, this teenager had never researched whether he had a realistic chance of receiving a significant financial aid package from Notre Dame. Some pricey schools are more generous than others. The teenager had also never considered less expensive alternatives. For instance, the University of Missouri, which has one of the finest journalism schools in the country, charges a fraction of the price. The mother, however, replied that this kid was only interested in "prestige" schools.

I mention this boy's dilemma because it's important to be flexible and realistic when you are hunting for colleges. Some of you can relate to this student's dream of attending Notre Dame. Who wouldn't want to boast about a university that makes others jealous? But the glow of attending a nationally prestigious school will surely fade when a graduate is overwhelmed by student debt and wondering if he'll be eating Cheerios for dinner on a regular basis.

This cautionary story illustrates this point: When your child begins hunting for colleges, price needs to be a consideration. If this isn't a focus from the start, you could ultimately end up telling a heartbroken child that you can't afford her $45,000-a-year dream school.

Focusing on price, however, absolutely does not mean squashing a child's dream. That's because college sticker prices are often irrelevant. Families that haven't saved much or even families that live comfortably with healthy six-figure incomes can find ways to cut the price dramatically if they just know where to look.

Answering the Financial Aid Question

How you begin your collegiate treasure hunt depends a great deal on whether you will receive need-based financial aid. At the start, it's critically important, therefore, that you determine whether your family will qualify for financial aid. Once you've figured that out, you will know what kind of schools to pursue. In the next chapter, you'll find the tools you'll need to determine whether financial aid is a possibility.

If You Do Qualify for Financial Aid...

You need to figure out which schools are generous and which are miserly. Many schools don't advertise their financial aid breakdowns of grants, loans, and work study, but as you'll learn later in the book, it is easy to retrieve financial aid statistics for individual schools.

The colleges and universities that often dangle the fattest financial aid packages are routinely the richest ones that sit on endowments that can reach into the billions of dollars. Recently 76 colleges and universities were sitting on endowments that were worth at least $1 billion. These schools are more likely to be able to bestow a kid with a free or heavily subsidized education.

Many of the schools with the most generous reputations, however, are also the hardest to wheedle your way into. Amherst College, for instance, says it will meet 100% of its students' financial needs. And even better, the school does not saddle its financial aid students with loans. Instead all Amherst students receive need-based grants. Princeton University in Princeton, New Jersey; Pomona College in Claremont, California; Davidson College in Davidson, North Carolina; Bowdoin College in Brunswick, Maine; and Williams College in Williamstown, Massachusetts, are also among the small, but growing number of elite schools that don't saddle families with loans.

Harvard, however, made everybody else's generosity look like a pittance when it announced its ambitious aid plan, which attracted front-page media attention. In addition to continuing to help middle-class and poor students, Harvard is now assisting families who make between $120,000 and $180,000 per year. The school caps the cost to these families at 10% of their income, which means the richest of these families will typically pay roughly $18,000 a year for a school with a recent price tag of $45,600. After Harvard's announcement, Yale University, Stanford University, and Brown University were among the schools that quickly followed with their own plans to benefit more affluent families.

It can't get much better than that, but, of course, there is a catch. Very few students can earn a spot in the freshman class at these schools. Amherst's acceptance rate is just 19%, and Davidson's is 30%. Harvard and Yale reject 91% of their applicants. Pomona turns away all but 18% of its applicants.

Luckily, plenty of schools do provide generous financial aid packages without requiring stratospheric SAT scores and valedictorian credentials. What's more, you can find schools that mix need-based financial aid with merit money, which is awarded regardless of whether a family is rich, poor, or in between. It's possible to obtain both kinds of assistance if you fit the profile that a particular school covets.

If You Don't Qualify for Financial Aid...

If "no" is the answer, you'll want to focus on the sugar daddies that award merit aid to students for academic achievements or other talents because the alternative is paying full fare.

As you'll learn in great detail later, tons of schools distribute merit aid without caring how much money mom and dad make or how much cash they have stuffed in bank accounts. The average merit award that private schools hand out slashes the tuition bill by 33.5%. Many public schools have also jumped on the merit aid bandwagon. And here's equally great news: Even "B" students can qualify for these awards at plenty of schools.

If you aren't receiving financial aid, you'll want to identify up front the schools that dispense merit awards, which are also known as tuition discounts. If you don't, you could end up spending tens of thousands of dollars more than you had planned.

Action Plan

Make it a priority to determine whether your family will qualify for need-based aid.

3

Using Financial Aid Tools

Always, always, always apply for financial aid even if you make $250,000 a year.

—Frederick E. Rugg, author of *Rugg's Recommendations on the Colleges*, 25th edition

When kids hit the teenage years, many families begin to worry about paying the college tab. It's about then that people start obsessing about financial aid. Parents who conclude that they didn't save enough start hoping that a fat aid package will magically materialize in their mail box. Others who have saved money worry that their industriousness will unfairly jeopardize their chances of qualifying for a handout.

Regardless of which families you most identify with, you probably harbor misconceptions about financial aid. One of the more common misconceptions is whether a family will qualify. Often, parents who are eligible for aid assume they won't be. Others who won't qualify for aid assume that schools will toss them a bone.

So how do you nail down whether your family will be eligible for financial aid? Ultimately, you will learn the verdict after you fill out the Free Application for Federal Student Aid or FAFSA. Even if the federal formula generates a grim verdict, you may still have a shot at help if you are applying to private schools. About 250 mostly private colleges and universities use an additional financial aid document, the CSS/Financial Aid PROFILE. The PROFILE uses much of the same data as the FAFSA, but it delves deeper into a family's finances.

You'll be taking a great risk if you wait to run the numbers until the real deadline for graduating high school seniors. As mentioned in

Chapter 2, "Looking for Cash in the Right Places," it's better to resolve the financial aid question before you ever start looking for appropriate academic and financial matches.

Federal Versus Institutional Methodology

Plenty of online calculators can help you get a good idea of whether you will be receiving financial aid in the future. If your child is a sophomore or junior in high school, you should run some preliminary numbers. If your child is just starting twelfth grade, you should make this a priority before your child starts applying to schools.

One tool you should check out is the federal government's FAFSA4caster (www.fafsa4caster.ed.gov). The FAFSA4caster calculates financial aid based only on the *federal methodology*. This is the methodology used to determine whether a family is eligible for federal money such as Pell Grants and subsidized Stafford Loans.

If you're considering private schools, you'll also need to play with another calculator. Some private institutions use an *institutional methodology* to determine who deserves assistance from their own discretionary pots of money. Private schools that use the PROFILE, which relies on the institutional methodology, are going to be nosier about your finances.

FinAid.org, which is an exhaustively comprehensive Web site about financial aid, is an excellent resource to plug in the institutional numbers. When you're at the site, click on the calculator link to find the Expected Family Contribution Calculator.

You can find another institutional calculator at CollegeBoard.com. At the site, type EFC calculator in the Search box.

When playing with these calculators, remember that financial circumstances change. For example, if you are trying out the FAFSA4caster when your daughter is in eleventh grade and months later you lose your job, those figures will no longer be accurate. All the results are going to be estimates until you type in the solid figures in the second half of your child's senior year in high school.

Getting the Results

These online tools aren't going to flash a green light if you can expect financial aid or a red light if you probably won't. It's a bit more involved than that. The software generates an *Expected Family Contribution* (*EFC*), which is presented as a dollar figure. This EFC is also what you will receive when the dry runs are over, and you complete the FAFSA and possibly the PROFILE.

The EFC represents what your family can afford to spend in one year on your child's college education. This dollar figure is generated after examining the parents' and the child's income and assets. It does not consider unsecured consumer debt, so it can be a fairly harsh assessment of a family's ability to pay.

Whether you will pocket any aid hinges greatly on the gap between your EFC and a school's price or, in higher ed lingo, the *cost of attendance*. The combination of the EFC and the so-called cost of attendance drives the financial aid process.

Schools define the cost of attendance differently. Some calculate it as the cost of tuition and room and board. Some also add the costs of books, transportation, and personal expenses. You can even find schools that use only tuition to determine the cost of attendance. The federal cost-of-attendance calculation is usually the one used to determine financial need.

This cost figure is critical because schools use the difference between a family's EFC and the cost of attendance to determine what a family's financial need is. Consequently, how much assistance a family can snag will be dramatically different if the school is modestly priced or breathtakingly expensive.

Suppose, for instance, your EFC is $15,000, and the in-state school your daughter wants to attend is $12,000. You'd be expected to pick up the entire collegiate tab because the school is cheaper than what the EFC indicates you can afford to pay. In contrast, if the school costs $40,000, you could end up with $25,000 in financial aid. In this scenario, you'd subtract your expected contribution of $15,000 from the $40,000 price tag.

Some families who didn't receive financial aid when they sent an older child to an in-state public university assume they won't get any money for a second or third child either no matter what school the child attends. But that assumption can be completely wrong. Being denied aid for a local public university that costs $8,000 doesn't mean the family won't receive aid for a school that costs $40,000. What's more, your EFC will be lower if you have more than one child attending college since the parent EFC contribution is divided by the number of children in college.

After you have a ballpark EFC, you can hone your college search to schools that could meet your need financially. If you will receive financial aid, look for generous schools that provide more need-based grant money than loans. If financial aid isn't a possibility, consider looking at in-state public institutions and/or private or out-of-state public schools that offer merit money.

Action Plan

Use a financial aid calculator to get an idea of whether you will ultimately receive financial aid. The verdict should influence what colleges you look at.

4

Financial Aid in the Real World

As you get toward the deadline of admitting your class, admissions offices panic. They just start throwing money at kids.

—Michael J. Rizzo, senior economist, American Institute of Economic Research

Somewhere in the Pacific Northwest, a single mom who makes her living waiting tables is having to schlep more dishes because of an elite East Coast school's false promises. The mother will have to work even harder to help pay back an obscene amount of loans that she must obtain to cover her talented daughter's college education that will cost close to $200,000.

The college in New York State had once seemed like a perfect fit. The school's lacrosse coach was excited about his West Coast recruit, and the girl, after a visit, became enchanted with the school. The college also appeared to be a perfect match financially since it states that it meets 100% of a student's financial needs.

But here's the part of the story that will make you ill. The school let it be known that the student would be admitted if she withdrew her financial aid application. In other words, the teenager was going to get squat from a school that's been showered with kudos for its generosity to needy students. When the teenager withdrew her aid application, the school didn't have to award her a financial aid package because technically she was no longer asking for it.

Despite the school's outrageous conduct, the girl enrolled at the school for the start of the 2007–2008 school year. How she and her mother will survive this financial body blow is anybody's guess.

Up until now, you might have thought that all that's necessary, if you qualify for financial aid, is to find the colleges and universities with the biggest hearts. Well not exactly. While the previous story is an extreme case (I hope), you need to steel yourself to be somewhat cynical of the financial aid process. The more you know about the practices of financial aid offices, and how they have evolved, the better your chances that you won't end up overwhelmed with debt. Knowing how the system works can also help you find affordable and wonderful schools that on the surface may seem far too expensive.

Here is one of the most important realities that you need to know about financial aid: Colleges don't treat every deserving family equally. You could have two applicants who were both raised by single mothers and who were both offered a spot in a school's freshman class. One of the kids is an "A" student with an above average SAT score, and the other is an "A-" student with an SAT score that's just a few measly points lower. According to the aid formula, both students need the same amount of money to attend. In this scenario, however, schools are often more likely to give a fatter aid package to the child with the better academic resume.

It's not hard to understand why this happens regularly. A college would prefer to fill its classes with "A" students rather than "A-" students. It's easy to argue that a high school senior who graduates with a 3.8 grade point average (GPA) is no more likely to become a successful adult than a student who leaves high school with a 3.6 GPA. Colleges obviously know this. Many schools, however, are obsessed with assembling ever more accomplished freshman classes on paper so they can elevate their rankings in the college guide books. And this desire can influence who gets the cash.

Colleges have to make choices because most of them don't have the kind of endowments that will allow them to meet the financial need of every child who gets accepted. If a school without a hefty endowment did provide enough money for every deserving applicant, the money would have to be tapped from elsewhere, which means there might be less cash to reduce class sizes, buy journals for the library, increase faculty pay, and hundreds of other needs.

At the same time, when word circulates about a particularly generous school, more teenagers who require a lot of assistance are likely to enroll. And that leaves fewer slots for affluent students, who are needed to pay the full fare. What's more, if a school is determined to help as many teenagers requiring assistance as possible, it might not offer merit money, which is awarded regardless of need to richer kids, who might go elsewhere if they don't get a break on their tuition.

In an article in its alumni magazine, Reed College in Portland, Oregon, commiserated with the financial aid dilemma Macalester College faced recently. More than 70% of the students attending the liberal arts college in St. Paul, Minnesota, were receiving financial aid under its "need-blind" policy, which doesn't factor in a student's ability to pay. But the financial strain became too much, and the school was forced to abandon it. "We were trying to find the right balance between quality and access," a Macalester administrator was quoted as saying. "Access is a really important value, but at some point you have to ask—'access to what?'"

When money becomes tight, colleges routinely offer some applicants aid packages that could only be described as moth eaten. This phenomenon happens so often that it has its own name—*gapping*. The school will accept a student, but the financial aid award is so low that the applicant will usually attend a different school. In some cases, the gap between what a family can afford and what the school offers can be tens of thousands of dollars. Other times, a child might be put on a financial aid waiting list.

Often the high school seniors in this category are middle-class and low-income students who are in the bottom half academically of the crop of teenagers who were accepted. Not all these students take the hint. Sometimes these kids decide to load up on crippling debt to attend their dream school. Before that happens, a school's financial aid officer will sometimes call the family to try to talk them out of committing financial suicide.

Is there something you can do with this insider intelligence to increase your chances of financial aid? Yes there is, and you'll find out in the next chapter.

Action Plan

If a school wants your child, the financial aid package will often be bigger.

5

A Peek Inside a Financial Aid Office

I hate to say no, but at some point you sometimes have to say, "It isn't going to work out." There are always some extremely disappointed families.

—Leslie Limper, director of financial aid, Reed College

While colleges and universities routinely grapple with their financial aid policies, very few agonize about it publicly. But that's what administrators at Reed College in Portland, Oregon, did when they discussed the school's financial aid evolution in a candid article that appeared in its alumni magazine.

Learning how Reed juggles the needs of its students with its own priorities can help families become more knowledgeable about how financial aid is parceled out at colleges and universities. Although every institution has developed its own system, plenty of schools rely on the so-called "need-aware" policy that Reed uses.

An apt description of Reed would be academic rebel. More than a decade ago, it told *U.S. News & World Report* to take a hike. It adamantly refuses to cooperate with the magazine's college rankings. You can't go to a football game at Reed because it shuns varsity sports. Students at this liberal arts college, which is surely one of America's most academic environs, spend a tremendous amount of time reading the classics.

Reed doesn't believe in luring wealthy kids to its picturesque campus by offering them money. In other words, while many colleges and universities offer smart and talented kids merit money, Reed scoffs at that carrot. It prefers dispensing the cash to smart students who couldn't attend the school without financial help.

Like other schools, what Reed does provide is need-based financial aid. The college, according to the article, budgets for about 140 freshmen—or 40% of the incoming class—to receive aid. In reality, about 53% of students at the school get some type of aid because some qualify after their freshman year. The average individual package for students is $29,950, and most of that comes from grants, which don't have to be repaid. Tuition and room and board at Reed was recently about $46,000.

Here's where the angst comes in: For years, Reed was on record as being a "need-blind" school that accepted applicants without being influenced by whether they could pay their own way. Despite the policy, a small number of needy kids who found themselves clinging to the bottom rungs of the school's acceptance ladder each year wouldn't receive money. In the article, the dean of Reed's faculty observed that the policy was "almost cruel" because it suggested that kids who were good enough for Reed were too poor to go.

The problem with maintaining a need-blind policy was that Reed's endowment couldn't sustain its charitable intentions. Only two or three dozen private schools, including the Ivies, are wealthy enough to offer a true need-blind program. And in reality, some of these schools accept students on a need-blind basis and then refuse to cough up the cash later.

Many of Reed's peers, such as Oberlin College in Oberlin, Ohio, and Carleton College in Northfield, Minnesota, which are elite liberal arts schools, use a "need-aware" policy. And that's what Reed ultimately embraced.

With Reed's need-aware policy, the admission staff ranks the applicants on a scale of one to five based on such factors as high school grades, extracurricular activities, diversity, alumni status, and what the school terms "potential."

Under this system, the most desirable students are admitted and offered financial packages based on their need. Not all the teenagers who receive aid, by the way, are impoverished. Half of the families report yearly incomes of more than $50,000.

During the admission process, the school doesn't start considering a family's financial capability until the aid budget is tapped out according to an in-house formula that tries to pinpoint how many accepted applicants will actually show up in the fall. The applicants who fall into the need-aware category and require financial assistance can be rejected. The policy typically hurts fewer than 100 students a year out of more than 3,000 who apply.

In talking about the policy in the article, Colin S. Diver, Reed's president, acknowledged it isn't perfect, but it was the best the school could devise for now. "We decided it was better to be open and admit to the fact that at some point we run out of money."

Action Plan

Keep in mind that the vast majority of schools don't enjoy unlimited financial resources. Consequently, it's important to look for schools that match a student's academic profile.

6

Winning the Financial Aid Lottery

It used to be that you could try for that reach school and if you got in, you didn't have to worry because everybody who got in, who needed money, got money. Today, however, as colleges are asked to fund more and more of their own operations with less and less assistance from the government, foundations, and families, they are increasingly reluctant to part with their money to enroll students who don't raise their academic profile.

—"The Real Deal on Financial Aid," Muhlenberg College Office of Admissions

Sometimes, a school wants a hot prospect so badly that it will twist its financial aid rules into a pretzel. That's got to be what happened when an elite West Coast school reeled in an exceptional student who just happened to be sitting on a $500,000 trust fund. A financial aid administrator could have run the numbers any way he wanted, but this teenager still wouldn't have qualified for need-based aid. But surprise, surprise, the private university, ignoring the trust fund, awarded him a yearly $30,000 aid package.

I mention this story not to make you more cynical about the financial aid process, but to alert you to one of the many ways that you can boost your chances of receiving more than crumbs from your favorite school. Whether you are a trust fund baby or far from it, here's what you need to do:

Always apply for financial aid. The best way to sabotage your chances for assistance is to assume that applying for need-based aid is pointless. Even families with six-figure incomes can qualify for a helping hand from more expensive schools. If you discover that your income far exceeds the income ceiling, you should still complete the forms because it could help your child secure a spot in the next freshman class.

This will sound crass, but some schools could be far more interested in your child after taking a peek at your finances. At some schools, an excellent candidate from a wealthy family will enjoy a better chance of being admitted over a promising student whose dad is on disability and whose mom works as a cashier. You may rightly believe that favoring an affluent student over a poor one is appalling, but plenty of schools make these sorts of decisions.

Skip the reach schools. If you're eager to capture a great financial aid package, reread the quote that starts this chapter. Muhlenberg College in Allentown, Pennsylvania, which is a school I greatly admire, posted on its Web site a remarkably candid portrayal about how schools award financial aid today. You can read the piece yourself by typing its title, "The Real Deal on Financial Aid," into Google's search engine.

One of the most important points that Muhlenberg's admissions office makes is that students who require financial aid need to focus on schools where they would be within the top one-third to the top one-quarter of the applicant pool. A child with a 3.2 GPA and a 1050 on the combined reading and math portion of the SAT shouldn't expect a financial aid windfall if the top 25% of students admitted into a particular school have an average GPA of 3.7 and a 1200 SAT. In fact, it's likely that this teenager's aid package would be stuffed with a work study opportunity and loans. In contrast, a teenager with a 3.8 GPA and a SAT of 1250 would be far more likely to receive a package that contains a large grant that doesn't have to be repaid.

If you're in the middle of the pack of kids accepted to a school, what you receive financially can depend on what else you'd bring to the institution. To break ties, schools will look at the extras. Are you a phenomenal volunteer in your community? Did you show leadership in your extracurricular activities? Are you from a state that's a 20-hour drive away? Are you a minority? Do you have special talents, such as music, art, or athletics?

A variety of online and printed sources provide individual schools' range of SAT scores and average GPA, which can help you compare your academic record with others. CollegeBoard.com and Petersons.com, for instance, provide both these statistics, as do various college guides that you can buy at a bookstore. You shouldn't assume, however, that any figures you see are the most current ones. Sometimes enrolled student scores are a couple years old and a school's standards might have risen since then.

Finding schools where you will be among the top bananas is a far cry from the approach that a lot of kids favor. Many students, as well as their parents, are eager to see how prestigious a school they can finagle their way into. Aiming for a reach school is fine if you don't mind when the financial aid office stiffs you. If you cringe at paying full price, include financial safety schools on your list.

Know where the money is. Some schools are more generous than others. The schools with the most money are typically private ones, which sit on their own institutional pots of financial aid. The Ivies and other wealthy schools have large endowments that allow them to provide generous aid packages. Schools that don't share the same star wattage but want to compete for high caliber students will sometimes ante up even more cash. They understand that some applicants will reject a fabulous financial package if an Ivy League institution welcomes them without giving up a dime.

In contrast, public schools typically don't have as much discretionary financial aid to toss around. At public schools, financial aid packages will often be filled with federal loans. Lower income families, whether they attend a private or a public school, will often qualify for a federal Pell Grant, which doesn't have to be repaid. Typically, these grants are reserved for families with income under $40,000. Public and private institutions will provide subsidized federal Stafford Loans to low to middle-income students. Eligibility is determined by a federal formula.

A student who doesn't qualify for a Pell or subsidized Stafford, can obtain a regular Stafford, while parents can take out a federal PLUS loan. Once again, you can obtain these regardless of whether the school is public or private. Unlike private schools, state institutions can't always offer financial aid beyond the federal program. Ironically, while families who expect their kids to go to state schools worry about being qualified for financial aid, the assistance will often be strictly loans.

Be leery of the numbers. If your child gets accepted into a school that brags that it meets 90% or 100% of its students' financial need, you may feel like celebrating. But hold off on the confetti. You need to know what's behind those numbers.

You're not going to be happy if a school meets 100% of your financial need with a package of loans. It's far better to find schools that back up their promises with grants, which don't have to be repaid.

You can learn whether a school is typically miserly or generous by looking at its profile on CollegeBoard.com. Once on the site, type the name of a college in the College QuickFinder and then click on the Cost & Financial Aid link. Using Muhlenberg College as an example, College Board indicates that the school meets 91% of a student's financial need. The breakdown was $19,116 in grants and $3,398 in loans.

Don't let the price tag fool you. Plenty of families assume that expensive schools are superior to cheaper ones. That belief is so pervasive that some schools have jacked up their prices to generate more foot traffic.

Higher tuition, however, doesn't mean that a school is sinking more cash into its academic programs. Some schools inflate their price as part of what insiders call the *Robin Hood admission strategy*. The school boosts its sticker price and then uses the excess cash to offer more assistance to the candidates it covets. While private schools use this strategy, some public colleges and universities try something similar for nonresident students. Often the out-of-state tuition is much higher at public universities, but a school will offer to cut the price in the form of a scholarship for the most desirable nonresidents.

In contrast, other schools, particularly those that serve a region, keep their prices lower and offer less financial aid because of the more reasonable cost of an education there. They use their cost advantage as a selling point.

Action Plan

You should enjoy better success at capturing a tuition price cut if you look for schools that represent a good academic fit.

7

Maximizing Financial Aid

Faced with backbreaking college costs, parents desperately try to appear impoverished for financial-aid purposes. But that is trickier than it seems.

—Jonathan Clements, former columnist at
The Wall Street Journal

To earn a spot in a respected college's freshman class, teenagers know the drill: Earn good grades and test scores and show schools that they are great students with promising futures. Despite all the years of preparation that precedes those coveted admissions letters, many families flunk at something that's also critically important: maximizing their chances for financial aid.

It's important to understand the basic rules because the financial aid system has perversely punished millions of conscientious parents. Two families could enjoy the same income and net worth and could have saved the exact same amount for college, but one could snag a fat financial award, and another could walk away with nothing but loans.

If you're puzzled about how you play the game, here are practical steps you can take to boost your chances of receiving a free handout:

Watch your financial footprints. Many parents assume that colleges aren't going to care about their family finances until their children are seniors in high school. That, however, is a dangerous assumption. You need to be mindful of any financial moves you make from sophomore year in high school through the senior year.

Schools are going to focus on your family's finances in the so-called *base year*, which refers to the calendar year prior to the year your child starts college. The base year for a child entering college in the fall of 2010, for example, would be 2009.

During this time period, you want to be extremely careful to avoid—if possible—any financial transactions that will jeopardize your chances at aid. Of course, if you've got a zero chance of qualifying for aid, you can ignore this advice.

Your aim should be to minimize the appearance of assets and income in this critical year. There are plenty of legal ways to pull this off. If you have credit card debt or a car loan, for instance, you may want to pay it down earlier than you'd contemplated. You could also contribute more to a retirement account. By doing these things, you'll have less cash on hand when financial aid officers start snooping. If you expect a year-end bonus, ideally you'll want to get it before the base year starts.

Once you're in that crucial base year, it's best to avoid selling profitable mutual funds, stocks, and other investments. The aid formula counts investment profits as income.

Don't touch retirement accounts. As long as the money stays in a retirement account, the vast majority of schools aren't going to care how much you've saved. You could have $5 million stockpiled in retirement accounts, and it wouldn't hurt your chances for financial aid. Some private colleges, however, may factor in your retirement accounts when calculating financial need. Any college or university, however, will take note if you tap into your retirement nest egg. Withdrawals from retirement accounts are considered income.

Another no-no is converting a traditional Individual Retirement Account (IRA) into a Roth IRA in the base year. Although a Roth conversion can make perfect sense as a retirement strategy, it could be a disaster if you're angling for financial aid. That's because the money that's moved from a traditional IRA into a Roth will be considered income.

Don't let up. Okay, you might be wondering what happens if you do all this for one year. Don't you need to file for financial aid at least three more years? That's true. The financial aid calculations are done annually, but the initial calculation can make the biggest impression. That said, you will unfortunately face the same challenges every year. Ideally, you'll want to use the strategies to obtain financial aid until roughly April of your child's junior year in college. By then you will have submitted your last financial aid application.

Pay attention to where the college money is kept. Unless you know that financial aid is an impossibility, be careful about where you stash the cash. That's because financial aid formulas treat children's assets far more harshly than the money that's in mom and dad's name.

It's easy to argue that treating one pot of money dramatically differently from another just because it's in a different type of account is ridiculous. After all, we're talking about one child's education whether parents saved the money or the child tucked away money from babysitting or cutting the lawn. The system is even more infuriating because the financial aid rules regarding various types of accounts keep changing. Imagine striking out the last batter in the World Series only to be told that it now requires four strikes to retire the hitter. That's what parents are up against.

So what are the rules? If you're going to qualify for financial aid, it's typically best to have the college money sitting in parental accounts. In the federal formula, the parents' assets will be assessed at no more than 5.64%. In contrast, a child's money will be assessed at 20%. Any cash sitting inside a custodial account belongs to the child. The most common custodial accounts are the Uniform Gifts to Minors Act (UGMA) and Uniform Transfer to Minors Act (UTMA).

Consider moving custodial cash. Luckily, there are ways to legally move cash out of custodial accounts. You don't have to wait until college to spend money in a traditional custodial account. You can dip into a custodial account to pay for summer camp, tutoring, or anything else that doesn't fall into the category of household needs such as the mortgage or food.

Parents can also transfer custodial money into a custodial 529 college plan. Custodial 529 accounts were traditionally treated like any other custodial cash for financial aid purposes, but no longer. Money in these accounts has absolutely no impact on financial aid calculations until July 2009. Starting July 1, 2009, custodial 529 plans will be reported as a parent asset if the student is a dependent.

Be an early bird. Imagine billions of dollars of financial aid money sitting in a feed trough, and you'll be able to appreciate why it's important to show up for breakfast early. It's a reality that each year's supply of discretionary financial aid will disappear. If many stellar kids apply months before you do, you might walk away only with loans because nothing else is left.

So what's early? You should file the FAFSA as soon after January 1 as possible, which is when the form becomes available. It's best if you file this form electronically because the software automatically detects common mistakes.

You may also have to file the CSS/Financial Aid PROFILE, the financial aid form used by hundreds of private schools. The PROFILE asks many of the same questions posed by the FAFSA, but it delves deeper into a family's financial picture. The PROFILE is available in October for the following year's freshman class. So if your child begins college in September 2009, you could fill out the form as early as October 2008.

To answer many of the questions on both the FAFSA and PROFILE, you'll need to pull numbers off your tax return. That's why it's critical to complete your tax return as soon as possible after January 1. You don't, by the way, have to file your tax return that early, you just have to have completed it and signed the document.

Of course, tackling taxes that early will seem impossible for many. After all, plenty of people may not get their W2 forms from their employers until mid January. Self-employed parents can have it even tougher since their tax returns can be more complicated and require gathering many more documents.

Luckily, there is a solution to this problem. You can file an estimated FAFSA. Because you're estimating the numbers you'll plug into the FAFSA, you should expect the schools to ask you for your signed income tax returns after it's filed. This approach also works with the PROFILE.

Pay attention to deadlines. If you miss a school's deadline for financial aid, your aid application might never be reviewed. Overlooking a financial aid deadline can be worse than missing a mortgage payment. Ask schools on your child's list about their financial aid dates.

Play the divorce card. In key ways, financial aid formulas treat the student of divorced parents differently. As far as the FAFSA is concerned, the noncustodial parent is irrelevant. The financial aid document doesn't even pose any questions about the other parent. The PROFILE does ask about the noncustodial parent, but the information is not taken into account when figuring a family's ability to pay. Ivy League schools do look at the noncustodial parent's assets and income when making aid decisions.

What can jeopardize a student's chances of walking away with financial aid is the remarriage of a custodial parent. The formula takes into account the assets and income of the stepfather or stepmother. Some newlyweds use a prenuptial agreement to try to block this, but they aren't successful.

Action Plan

To boost your chances of financial aid, you need to start planning well in advance of your child's high school graduation.

8

Maximizing Financial Aid, Part II

The (financial aid) formula is definitely showing its age. A lot of today's realities weren't contemplated by lawmakers when they designed the formula.

—Mark Kantrowitz, publisher of FinAid.org

While talking to a friend one afternoon I watched her work herself into a tizzy about her inability to qualify for financial aid. She hadn't even applied yet, but she had convinced herself that her daughter's chances of getting a free handout were zilch. When I asked the stay-at-home mom why, she explained that the family had a decent amount of cash stuffed in retirement accounts, and her small home had jumped considerably in value over the years. Ironically, I suspect her family would have qualified for aid.

There are a lot of misconceptions about financial aid—starting with who qualifies. If you're hoping to maximize your chances of pocketing financial aid dollars, you should know what's out there for families like your own. As mentioned in an earlier chapter, the best way to get a verdict is to use an online calculator at FinAid (www.finaid.org) or the College Board (www.collegeboard.com).

Beyond cranking out your own numbers, looking at figures compiled by the U.S. Department of Education's National Postsecondary Student Aid Study should be illuminating. In the study, the federal statisticians broke down the percentage of undergraduates receiving financial aid into six different income categories—the highest category contained families making at least $100,000, and the lowest were families earning less than $20,000.

More than 76% of the poorest families received federal assistance, while 39% of the wealthiest parents did. But this doesn't tell the whole story. More than 73% of the poorest families received federal grants, which don't have to be repaid, compared to 1% of the most affluent parents. And they weren't the only ones shut out of federal grants. The percentage of families making between $60,000 and $79,000 who received federal grants was 3.7%.

Nearly all the federal aid that families with annual incomes of $60,000 or more received was via loans. Consequently, it's important to understand that if you're hoping for federal financial aid and you make $60,000 or up, you will be angling for loans. Even families earning between $40,000 and $59,999 had difficulty qualifying for federal grants—just 21.5% in the study snagged one. This is obviously depressing news, but it's better to know it now.

Affluent families will experience better luck if they aim for institutional financial aid, which schools dispense using their own criteria. While public schools have some discretionary money, it's the private schools that dole out much of it. What's amazing—and what financial aid critics would condemn as despicable—is that wealthy families enjoy just about as much chance of nabbing institutional grants as the desperately poor kids. According to the federal study, nearly 29% of families in the top income category received institutional grants versus 36% for those in the lowest bracket. About 34% of families earning anywhere from $40,000 to $99,999 pulled in grants too.

Here is the take-home message: If you want need-based grants, private schools or public schools that are aggressively trying to boost their *U.S. News & World Report* rankings are good places to look.

Armed with this knowledge, here are two more ways to boost your chances of financial aid:

Fill out the FAFSA. All parents should submit the Free Application for Federal Student Aid (FAFSA) because their children won't be eligible for federal or state aid without it. Wealthy parents sometimes skip this exercise because they figure it's pointless. Some schools, however, will not award merit scholarships unless families have jumped through the financial aid hoop. This can be required even though these awards are supposed to be based on academics, student talents, or some other criteria that have nothing to do with family finances. If your child is applying to a school that uses the CSS/Financial Aid PROFILE, submit that one too.

Know what assets count in aid calculations. Ironically, families who qualify for aid frequently assume that they won't, and families who won't get a handout assume they will. A lot of the confusion arises from what jeopardizes a person's chances for aid.

Like my friend, many parents assume that they will be disqualified if they possess substantial retirement accounts. Only a small fraction of schools, however, are interested in cash that's stashed in these accounts.

Actually, most families won't even be penalized for the money saved in other types of investments either. Federal aid rules permit families to shield cash from the aid formula by using the so-called Asset Protection Allowance. How much money you can shield depends on whether a household has one or two parents and the age of the oldest parent. Here is an example from the 2008–2009 school year: If a student lives with both parents and the oldest parent is 51, the family is entitled to an allowance of $50,500. If the oldest parent is 49, the allowance drops to $47,900.

You can find the current Asset Protection Allowance table by visiting the Federal Student Aid site at http://studentaid.ed.gov/. Once there, click on Tools and Resources and then click on Publications. The table is published in an annual document entitled the *EFC (Expected Family Contribution) Formula* that's updated yearly. The EFC represents what a school will expect your family to pay toward one year of your child's education.

The PROFILE's asset protection formula, which is based on the consumer price index, is slightly different. Regardless of which formula is used, only a small fraction of families have their EFC hiked because of parent investments.

Here's another common misconception: We're sure to get rejected because our house is worth too much. This is a frequent fear on the West and East Coasts and other places where real estate values are high. But here's the good news: the FAFSA doesn't give a hoot about your house. You could live in an oceanfront mansion in Malibu or a one-bedroom lean-to without running water, and it makes no difference because the FAFSA doesn't even inquire about the family residence.

Many private schools, however, will be curious about the value of your home. But even so, home equity is unlikely to jeopardize aid for many families because colleges typically cap the figure.

Action Plan

- Regardless of your income, always apply for financial aid.
- Understand what assets count in the aid formulas.

9

Appealing the Verdict

To me and my colleagues, this year it's all about "the buck." I understand this and accept it, of course, but after hearing "College X gave me more money; what can you do?" for the 100th time, I begin to wonder if anyone is listening to our messages, and if anyone really cares about value.

—Robert J. Massa, vice president for enrollment and college relations, Dickinson College

What happens if your family doesn't get enough financial aid? Perhaps the price tag for the college your child wants to attend is $35,000 and the school awarded your child a $10,000 merit scholarship. A nice gesture, you might think, but certainly not enough.

Don't give up. It is sometimes possible to squeeze more cash out of a school that clearly wants your child to be in its latest crop of freshmen. Here's what you need to do:

Skip the tears. Financial aid officers hate to see parents cry or shout or in anyway show the kind of emotions that would make them want to run out of the room or hang up the phone. They hate histrionics. Instead, you should talk dispassionately when you request that the school reexamine its aid package. You can make this request by phone, in person, or by mail. Don't send a letter or e-mail until you know to whom to address the correspondence. If you hear nothing after a week, follow up with a call.

Provide a number. When making your appeal, don't dwell on how wonderful your son or daughter is. Aid officers are immune to parental bragging since they've heard it all before—hundreds or thousands of times. The schools also don't want to hear you complain that the school costs too much. Colleges know that, but they keep receiving plenty of applications, and many families aren't going to quibble about the price.

Rather than try these futile approaches, provide the school with concrete numbers to work with. Let a school know how much more money you realistically need and how much you could afford to borrow. Be as specific as possible and provide documentation. For example, you might want to provide the school a cash flow-analysis done by an accountant.

Don't overlook extenuating circumstances. It's up to you to alert a school's financial aid officer to circumstances that might boost the package. For instance, the federal financial aid form, commonly referred to as FAFSA, doesn't provide space to mention that a family member is disabled and has high medical bills. There is also nowhere on the form to note that parents are taking care of an aging parent or that the family's stocks got pummeled in recent months or that a higher than usual salary included a one-time bonus.

Also, after a family completes the financial aid applications, plenty can change. It's up to you to notify the school—no matter where you are on the financial aid timeline. If a parent loses a job, dies, becomes disabled, or divorces, let the college know.

Try leverage. Let's suppose your child received great financial packages from other schools, but the college where he or she is aching to attend wasn't nearly as generous. If this happens, contact the college with the punier package and explain that your child received higher offers elsewhere. Don't gloat about the better awards or act indignant that the school wasn't as generous from the outset. You should absolutely resist using the word "negotiate." Colleges hate the "N" word. Just explain that your child would really love to attend the school, but the financial strain would be far less elsewhere.

For this strategy to have any chance of working, however, the schools have to be competing for the same universe of kids. An aid officer at Case Western Reserve University in Cleveland, for instance, isn't going to be impressed if your child earned a merit scholarship from a school in rural Oklahoma. But Case Western Reserve could become interested if the other offers came from its natural competitors such as Carnegie Mellon University, Rensselaer Polytechnic Institute, and the University of Rochester.

Reexamine your paperwork. When filling out financial aid applications, mistakes happen. In fact, by one estimate 90% of families make a mistake when they complete the FAFSA. Slipped decimal points, transcribed figures, and other mishaps occur frequently. Some parents leave a question blank instead of inserting a zero. The wrong Social Security number is typed in or parents supply the monthly income instead of yearly. If you're disappointed or surprised by your child's aid package or lack of one, reexamine your figures.

It's not just parents who goof up. Errors can occur when institutions process thousands of applications on tight deadlines. So if an aid verdict seems crazy, it might very well be. That's what happened to one student, who received significant financial aid packages from Dartmouth College and Tufts University, but he got zilch from Yale University. The family submitted copies of the aid offers from the other schools and ultimately was rewarded for taking that extra step. Yale had overlooked something in its financial assessment and corrected the oversight by producing its own award package.

Use a calculator. Excellent calculators are located at FinAid, the comprehensive online financial aid resource (www.finaid.org/calculators/), that can help you evaluate financial aid packages. The Simple Award Letter Comparison Tool allows you to compare packages from three schools and highlights the differences in the cost of attending each of them. The Advanced Award Letter Comparison Tool provides a more in-depth analysis.

Another resource is FinancialAidLetter.com, which was co-created by a senior writer at *U.S. News & World Report* while she was enrolled in a fellowship program.

Disappearing cash. Some schools are most generous to their incoming freshmen. But what happens when the students are sophomores or juniors, and the school knows it has a captive audience? After the freshman year, some institutions will start shifting their aid package more toward loans rather than grants, which don't have to be repaid. To protect yourself, ask the financial aid office whether you can expect the same amount of aid in the same proportion of loans and grants during all four years. This will assume, of course, that your own financial circumstances don't change.

Action Plan

- Double check aid applications for mistakes.
- Try appealing if you receive a disappointing aid package.

Part II

Capturing Tuition Discounts

10

The Race for Cash

How admissions offices contrive to meet all these institutional needs—how they manage to enroll pre-meds, painters, children of alumni ("legacies"), soccer players, Exeter grads, and African-Americans in roughly the same proportions, year after year—while maintaining (or improving) the college's median S.A.T. score is a good story, and it's made better by the understandable reluctance of most colleges to speak frankly about the process.

—Louis Menand, *The New Yorker* magazine

One spring, a friend of mine in Los Angeles called in a panic. Her bright daughter had recently received acceptance letters from the University of California in Berkeley, as well as the San Diego campus, which are extremely tough schools to get into. Sarah Lawrence College, a well-respected liberal arts school in New York, had also sent her good news.

So what was the problem? My friend's daughter, Jenny, had decided she wanted to spend her next four years at a liberal arts college, but Sarah Lawrence hadn't offered any cash. And the family needed more than just a bunch of loans to seriously consider a private school.

The deadline to apply at most schools was just days away, but I suggested they quickly look elsewhere. Jenny, who is an aspiring actress, wants to major in theater so they ended up considering some schools, which I knew offered merit money to talented kids. Jenny ultimately applied to Muhlenberg College in Allentown, Pennsylvania, and Lawrence University in Appleton, Wisconsin, which are known for their excellent theater programs.

Muhlenberg, as well as Lawrence, offered Jenny generous aid packages. In fact, she received so much cash from Muhlenberg, where she ultimately decided to attend, that it's costing the family several thousand dollars *less* each year to attend the $41,000 Pennsylvania school than if she had chosen Berkeley (price tag: roughly $21,000 for state residents).

Muhlenberg became affordable thanks to a collegiate practice that some have loudly vilified, and others have vigorously defended. Jenny is attending her first choice because she received a large helping of merit money. And there is no reason why you can't score the same sort of merit windfall if you know where to look.

Merit money is different from other sorts of financial aid because a student doesn't need to qualify for financial assistance to capture it. The kids of hedge fund managers or celebrities can qualify for merit money, which the higher education industry calls *tuition discounts*. You'll also see merit money referred to as non-need-based aid. In fact, affluent kids are often more likely to win merit awards than a child of a single mom who must work two jobs. And, as you learn in Chapter 11, "The Inside Scoop on Merit Money," that last reality has helped to generate a lot of the booing and hissing from certain academic corners.

In the old days, schools reserved their merit scholarships for just a handful of the most brainiac students. A National Merit Scholar, who strayed into an admissions office, could probably snag an award, but mere mortal students either paid full price or obtained need-based financial aid.

In the early 1990s, however, colleges and universities started enticing more kids with merit money. And, curiously enough, it wasn't just the private colleges that sit on healthy endowments that were dispensing merit awards like Halloween candy. Public universities, eager to lure smart kids, some living a time zone or two away, started doing the same thing.

Today, most schools will discount their tuition to the kids they really want. And the discounts are substantial. According to the College Board, the average tuition discount that private four-year colleges and universities award is 33.5%. So if a school's tuition is $25,000, and a freshman got the average discount, the bill would shrink to $16,625. The average price cut at four-year public institutions, which typically charge lower tuition, is 14.7%. The discounts at public schools tend to be the most generous at smaller institutions, as well as at universities with larger out-of-state populations.

These average tuition breaks only begin to hint at how freely the money is flowing. At schools that are aggressive dispensers of merit money, such as the University of Rochester, Case Western Reserve University, Tulane University, Catholic University of America, Southern Methodist University, University of Tulsa, University of Dayton, and Baylor University, just about one out of every three freshmen were recently snagging merit money. At Tulane, the average merit award was recently more than $19,000 a pop.

The percentage of kids who win merit money is just as staggering at some public universities. At the University of Florida, 57% of its students recently pocketed merit awards, while the University of South Carolina singled out 34% of its kids for tuition discounts. At the University of Virginia, fewer students capture merit money (13%), but the average award of more than $9,000 is a jaw-dropping sum for a public institution. Nipping at Virginia's heels is the University of Alabama where more than one out of five students were getting merit cash with the average award at more than $8,500. Miami University in Oxford, Ohio, however, makes these generous public schools look like misers. The state school was recently giving merit cash to 39% of its kids, and the average award was $11,864.

Financial goodies are hardly reserved exclusively for "A" students. Every school maintains its own criteria for merit money. At some institutions, for instance, a child might qualify for academic scholarships with a 3.0 GPA and an SAT score barely above 1000 on a scale of 1600. At far more selective colleges, the money spigot might get turned on if a child has a 3.8 GPA and an SAT above 1350.

One easy way to find schools that offer scholarships that match a teenager's profile is to use Google. Just type in the SAT score (combined reading and math) that's close to your child's score, such as 1000, 1050, 1070, 1100, 1120, and on up or plug in your child's ACT such as 25, 26, and on up. You'll be amazed at how many hits you'll get. When I typed "scholarships" and "1050 SAT" into Google, I got 689 hits. When I searched for "scholarships" and "1200 SAT," I received 2,790 hits.

Even kids with a blemished academic record might be able to find cash if they possess something that a school wants. For instance, so-so grades will be less of an issue for teenagers applying to music conservatories, where auditions will often be the key factor. A kid with incredible leadership skills or a teenage entrepreneur who started a business in his messy bedroom can find schools eager to talk.

Merit decisions can also hinge on a school's latest academic focus. A school emphasizing its fine arts program, for instance, could be excited to find talented sculptors and painters. As you'll learn later, even a kid's gender can provide a leg up on merit awards.

At this point, you may be wondering why schools are throwing money at kids who won't necessarily need it. You'll find out why in the next chapter and then you'll learn how to pinpoint schools with the big hearts.

Action Plan

- Don't assume that you must pay full price for a college education.
- Look for schools that offer discounts for desirable students.

11

The Inside Scoop on Merit Money

Subsidizing the education of well-off smart kids isn't going to get us where we need to go—more students enrolled in college, more students graduating from college, and fewer students finishing their degrees with debilitating loads of debt.

—Lindsey Luebchow, New America Foundation

So why are so many colleges and universities handing out merit money to students who don't necessarily need help? Here's the short, cynical answer: Higher education has gone Hollywood.

Collegiate players don't get to bask at their own Oscar award ceremony, but their reward is just as coveted. Their academic calendars are marked for one big day every year when *U.S. News & World Report* releases its newest rankings of the nation's colleges and universities.

For colleges, a high ranking is better than a gold-plated statue. In fact, even a slight up-tick in a school's ranking can trigger a delirious celebration, while a demotion can create anguish and despair within a school's academic inner sanctum.

Because the stakes are so high, some schools spend millions on self-improvement projects aimed at impressing the magazine's editors. (No lie!) Some administrators are even personally rewarded if the verdict is a good one.

This is what explains the ratings obsession: Teenagers and their parents now consider *U.S. News & World Report*'s annual college publication the higher ed Bible. Families use it as a shortcut to judge the quality of individual schools, and they often express greater interest in schools with stellar ratings. This phenomenon leads to more kids applying to ratings winners or institutions that have noticeably improved in this numbers game. This then allows the lucky institutions to reject more applicants. And turning away more kids can then help these schools boost their ratings even higher. This silly cycle never ends.

When a college or university is intent on leapfrogging over its competitors, an excellent way to pull this off is to stack its team with ringers. A school accomplishes this by assembling the best crop of freshmen possible, at least as measured by *U.S. News & World Report's* controversial methodology. And promising merit money is one sure-fire way to lure promising applicants to a campus.

The use of merit awards isn't actually as simple as I've described it. In fact, the internal process that schools undertake to achieve the optimum mix of revenue spent to freshmen bought has its own name: *enrollment management*. Campus enrollment managers, sometimes with the help of outside consultants, will often use the cash in their own institutional kitties to shape their incoming classes to meet their own academic and financial goals.

The best article I've seen on enrollment management—a practice that schools would prefer to keep hidden—was written by Matthew Quirk in the November 2005 issue of *The Atlantic*. You can read the illuminating article at the magazine's Web site (www.theatlantic.com) by typing in its title: "The Best Class Money Can Buy."

If you're a parent with a smart child, the use of merit money will seem like a promising and equitable development. With the cost of college so obscene, why should any parents pay full price?

It's a sentiment that I can completely identify with. In fact, when my daughter, my husband, and I went shopping for schools, most of the institutions on our list dispensed merit money. The merit scholarships my daughter was offered allowed her to ultimately attend her No. 1 pick—a liberal arts college in Pennsylvania—for close to the same price at the premier public universities in California where we live.

The downside of merit money is that at some schools it can drain coffers reserved for need-based financial aid. This is the cash used for deserving kids who must cross colleges off their list if they don't receive considerable financial help.

In the past, plenty of schools were more willing to hand out full scholarships to the neediest kids. But today many institutions are more likely to take what would have been, say, a $30,000 need-based financial aid package and divide it into three or four merit awards. The school offers these awards of $7,500 or $10,000 a piece to more affluent students with solid test scores, which can help with the college's rankings and bring in more revenue. Merit awards of this size can often seal the deal with families who are determined to pocket some sort of discount. Enrollment consultants can sometimes even predict how much cash it will take to attract certain categories of kids to a particular school.

The Education Sector, which is an independent educational think tank in Washington, DC, blasted this practice in a report that examined financial aid practices at 50 state flagship universities. "There's a ruthless bottom-line logic driving this trend," the report concluded. "Poor students bring in far less net revenue than rich ones and do nothing to burnish an institution's status in the higher education marketplace."

Gordon Winston, a professor emeritus at Williams College and the director of The Williams Project on the Economics of Higher Education, was even less diplomatic with his assessment. In the *Atlantic* article he observed that enrollment management is "a brilliantly analytical process of screwing the poor kids." In another publication, Winston insisted that "enrollment managers are ruining American higher education."

The merit aid stampede by public universities that are also gunning for higher ratings from *U.S. News & World Report* has especially alarmed critics. According to Education Trust, the amount of grant aid awarded to families earning at least $100,000 jumped 406% between 1995 and 2003, while cash given to poverty-stricken families making less than $20,000 dropped 13%.

It also explains why I wasn't surprised when I talked to the father of a bright teenager in New Hampshire for a college story that I wrote for *BusinessWeek*. He told me that his daughter, who was a National Merit Scholarship finalist, had been courted—out of the blue—by the University of Florida and the University of Oklahoma, which were both offering her full-ride scholarships. Knowing this, it wasn't startling when the annual *Chronicle of Higher Education Almanac 2007–2008* noted that the University of Florida had lassoed more freshman National Merit Scholarship winners (257) than all others schools except Harvard University (294). The University of Oklahoma (140) and Rice University tied for fourteenth on the list and beat out several Ivy League schools.

Here's another dubious development: Certain schools have jacked up their price, in part, because some families won't take a school seriously unless it costs as much as other comparable schools. A *New York Times* article shared the story of Ursinus College in Collegeville, Pennsylvania, which raised its tuition and fees 17.6% one year after the board concluded that it was losing applications because families thought the tuition was too low. After the school raised its tuition, it received nearly 200 more applications the next year. To soften the blow, Ursinus increased its student aid nearly 20%.

The article noted that other schools, such the University of Notre Dame, Bryn Mawr College, Rice University, the University of Richmond, and Hendrix College also sharply increased their tuition for competitive reasons while boosting their financial aid.

The critics of merit money practices typically direct their frustrations at colleges and universities not the families who are angling for price breaks. Even so, what often gets lost in discussions among industry insiders is this: Merit money wouldn't be so critical to so many families if the cost of college wasn't continually outstripping the rate of inflation and the average mom and dad's salary. Even a family that makes \$100,000 or \$150,000 a year is going to have digestive troubles choking down a \$30,000 bill that comes due every September.

Ironically, one reason for runaway tuition at some schools is because they need a steady stream of cash to provide merit money to the kids they most covet.

If you won't qualify for need-based financial aid, it makes perfect sense to find a school that is not only an academic match but also one that will reward you for sending your child there. If not, you could end up paying full price and subsidizing somebody else's luckier kid. I can't imagine anybody wanting to be caught in that position.

Action Plan

- There are many more opportunities to capture a merit award than in the past.
- If your family doesn't have a shot at need-based aid, look for schools that hand out merit aid.

12

Academic Freebies

The golden rule is this: If you don't ask, you won't get the money. You should never assume that you won't get any.

—Rick Darvis, CPA, cofounder of the National Institute of Certified College Planners

During the height of the college mating season, my daughter received a piece of mail from Beloit College, a wonderful liberal arts school in Wisconsin that listed its merit scholarships. The mailer contained a laundry list of Beloit's awards that ranged from $4,000 a year to free tuition. Beloit was quite specific about who qualifies for this free cash. For a top scholarship, for instance, the school was looking for kids with an unweighted grade point average of at least 3.5, or they could be among the top 10% of their class. The school also required an SAT score of at least 1220 (on a 1600 scale) or an ACT score of 27.

There was nothing extraordinary about this scholarship notice. My daughter received countless mailings from colleges, solicited and unsolicited, that outlined their respective scholarship opportunities. That frankly is the point. Merit awards have become a ubiquitous partner in today's courtship between colleges and high school students. Increasingly the question to ask is not, "Do you offer merit scholarships?," but rather, "How generous are the ones that you provide?"

Merit money is particularly important to families that don't qualify for financial aid. But students who qualify for need-based financial aid, are also eligible. If you'd like a shot at capturing some of this money, here's how to increase your chances:

Find the right fit. Don't make the same mistake as the prosecutor who tried to convince a jury to convict O.J. Simpson of murder. To bolster his case, the prosecutor asked the ex-football star to try on the notorious bloody glove without knowing what would happen. Of course, as we all know, the glove didn't fit—legal experts suggested it had shrunk from the blood. And the chances for conviction withered right before the courtroom television cameras.

So what does this have to do with you and your teenager? I'd suggest that a teenager should never apply to a college without already having a good idea of what the admissions committee is going to say about his or her application. But more importantly, you should also pretty much know what kind of financial package the school will ultimately award your child. With the higher ed price tag so exorbitant, you could be committing economic suicide if you don't narrow your search to schools that you believe will be generous to your child. In fact, one of the initial questions that you should ask when looking at a university's or college's glossy marketing material is this: How likely is it that this school will extend a price break?

Know where to look for cash. A quick way to discover whether a school awards merit money is by looking at college profiles on the College Board's Web site (www.collegeboard.com). Type the name of the school into the Web site's College QuickFinder. Once you've pulled up a school's profile, click on the Cost & Financial Aid link. This section includes the institution's "average non-need-based aid" per recipient. This is another term for merit money. If you see a blank in this space, that's an excellent tip-off that a school doesn't dispense merit awards.

What the College Board's Web site won't tell you is what percentage of the freshman class wins merit awards and what it takes to get one. You can often find the answer to one or both of those questions by visiting a school's Web site. I'm using Case Western Reserve University in Cleveland as an example because it's a school that aggressively awards merit cash.

According to the College Board, Case Western Reserve's average merit award is $16,174. Armed with that information, I visit the school's Web site and learn that more than 93% of first-year students receive some type of financial aid. The average financial aid package is $26,989, while the cost of tuition and room and board is roughly

$44,000. The percentage of incoming students who snag a merit award is 61%. The average award is $18,590. The school's own figure is more generous than the College Board's, which is why it's good to double check outside figures.

The private school doesn't provide many details on how you qualify for this money, but the Web site does explain that even Bill Gates' kid could qualify for a scholarship since financial income is irrelevant. The admissions office states that scholarships are awarded to students considered above average in the applicant pool, and it mentions that SAT or ACT scores provide one measure. The school also notes, however, that scores are only one measure, so many students submitting scores below the median also receive scholarships.

Because standardized test scores are factored in, you would want to take a look at Case Western Reserve's range of SAT scores. For that piece of the puzzle, head back to the school's profile on the College Board's Web site and click on the SAT link. The College Board publishes the middle 50% range of the critical reading, math, and writing sections of the test. Few schools, at this point, appear to be using the writing scores. At Case Western Reserve, the middle 50% of the school's freshmen scored between 600 and 700 on the critical reading section and scored between 630 and 730 on the math section. That means, for instance, that the bottom quarter of the class scored below 600 on reading, and the top 25% of the class received a score higher than 700.

Go to the source. You can track a school's financial aid footprints by checking its Common Data Set. Each year, colleges and universities compile this gold mine of statistics that includes information on financial aid, as well as graduation rates, freshman class profile, student retention, and many other areas.

The format for any school's Common Data Set is identical, which makes comparisons of different institutions a snap. If you get your hands on this document, you'll obtain far more data than you would get curling up with any college guide. An easy way to find a school's Common Data Set is to Google the term, as well as the school's name. You can also type "Common Data Set" into a college's search engine. To illustrate what you can find in the Common Data Set, I'm going to use Juniata College in Huntingdon, Pennsylvania, which is my daughter's school. I picked Juniata because it provides most of its students with both need-based financial aid and merit scholarships.

For this exercise, I headed to Juniata's five-page financial aid section within the Common Data Set. Here's what I learned: Of the 388 freshmen in a recent Juniata class, 347 students applied for need-based aid. The school concluded that 310 students or 89% qualified for need-based aid. Of that number, 304 freshmen received need-based grants that didn't have to be repaid. For the freshman class, the average financial aid package was $18,763. Tuition and room and board at the school that year was roughly $35,000.

What parents will want to know is whether the average financial aid package contains a bunch of loans or whether it provides valuable grants. Juniata reported that the average loan that its frosh financial aid recipients received was $3,448 or 18% of the typical package. So for this school, most of the aid is the desirable kind.

What I also learned by looking at Juniata's figures is that most of the kids who received financial aid also captured merit money. In fact, 278 students of those who qualified for need-based financial aid also received merit money. In addition, 72 students, who were too affluent to qualify for need-based aid, received merit awards that averaged $12,358. The figures Juniata provided for its other students were similar to the freshmen statistics.

When you use these figures, it's much easier to calculate whether a school will be affordable. If your son or daughter has assembled a list of potential schools, print out the Common Data Set for each one of them. Only after comparing the generosity of schools and their requirements for merit money and financial aid, can you form a pretty good idea of whether these schools make financial sense or whether the hunt should continue.

Action Plan

- Investigate how generous a school is by looking at its Common Data Set numbers.
- A quick place to look for financial aid numbers is the College Board's Web site.

13

Creating a Buzz

It's almost taken for granted, no matter who you are, that you're going to get some kind of discount.

—Bruce G. Hammond, director of college counseling, Sandia Preparatory School in Albuquerque

When a Certified Public Accountant from upstate New York, contemplated how he was going to pay for his son's college, he knew he didn't want to pay the sticker price. The son was a good student though he wasn't brilliant. But the CPA, who advises his own clients about their college options, figured that if he proceeded strategically, his son would win a tuition discount.

As the father and son started searching for colleges, they made sure the list contained good academic fits that were located in different regions. He ultimately applied to five schools—Lynchburg College in Lynchburg, Virginia; Seattle (Washington) University; Hartwick College in Oneonta, New York; West Virginia University; and the State University of New York at Albany. The father and son included the in-state school because they reasoned that a private school is more likely to award money if it understands that a child's fall-back option is inexpensive.

The teenager won merit scholarships at all the private schools on his list, including Hartwick College where he enrolled. "If we had not done any planning at all," the CPA recalled, "we would have had a big college bill."

If your desire to avoid college sticker shock is equally strong, here are other ways to avoid getting stuck with the entire bill:

Create a buzz. Some schools can become more magnanimous if they know that their competitors are interested in the same student. The University of Rochester, for example, might be more interested in a talented student who is also being courted by some of its rivals, such as Carnegie Mellon University in Pittsburgh, Case Western Reserve University in Cleveland, and Rensselaer Polytechnic Institute in Troy, New York. Sometimes rivals are scattered across the country, while others may share an athletic conference. Your child doesn't have to be a jock to try this strategy. Here's why: Schools that compete on the soccer field, baseball diamond, or football field hate seeing their competition stealing away top prospects, whether a child is a baritone, a photographer, a computer genius, or just a wonderful student.

So how do you know what a school's academic peers are? For starters, you can ask college admissions offices and your high school counselor. College resource guides are another resource. The *Princeton Review's The Best 366 Colleges*, for example, includes in each school's profile, institutions that applicants also look at. For instance, the profile of the University of Puget Sound in Tacoma, Washington, says that students sometimes prefer Colorado College in Colorado Springs, Colorado; Lewis & Clark College in Portland, Oregon; Willamette University in Salem, Oregon; and Whitman College in Walla, Walla, Washington.

On the College Board's Web site, the profile of individual schools lists competitors that students have also researched. For instance, the College Board snapshot of St. Louis (Missouri) University, a private Jesuit institution, recently noted that students who looked at St. Louis University also checked out Marquette University in Milwaukee, Loyola University in Chicago, Vanderbilt University in Nashville, and Washington University in St. Louis.

How will competing schools know where your child is applying? They will find out by looking at the application you submit for federal financial aid. On your Free Application for Federal Student Aid (FAFSA), you will list other schools that you'd like the form sent to.

Explore other time zones. Admissions officers get excited when they receive applications from distant places. Plucking kids from Texas, California, or Maine, for example, can help a college in the Midwest or the South boost its geographic diversity. Applying to schools far from your home can give you a leg up on merit money decisions. If an admissions officer at a Pennsylvania college is trying to decide who gets a scholarship between two equally talented candidates, do you think he or she would give it to a kid who lives 50 miles down the road or to somebody from San Francisco? That's not a hard one to answer.

Consult your high school guidance counselor. Counselors should know what schools have been particularly generous to graduates at your child's high school. Also ask the counselor whether your school uses Family Connection from Naviance. This is an incredible online service that is customized to individual high schools. The online program allows teenagers to see how successful the previous graduating classes at their own high school have been in the admission process. With Family Connection, which is password protected, a student can look at the standardized test scores and grade point averages of alumni and learn which academic records were good enough to gain an acceptance and which were rejected. A scatter plot shows which students—their names are withheld—got into a particular college or university and which failed. If your high school doesn't offer Family Connection, lobby for it.

Research a school's wish list. Learn more about the kind of students a school covets by curling up with its mission statement and strategic plan. (Look for these documents on a school's Web site.) Reading a mission statement can give you a better idea of what a school values most in educating its students. If its value resonates with you, you could be a better candidate and a happier camper during the next four years.

The strategic plan can provide clues on what the school would like to do in the future. If the school says it wants to put more emphasis on sciences—and it's gearing up to build a new science building—chemistry and biology majors should take note. Likewise, a school that says it wants to focus on creating a more diverse campus or attracting more out-of-state students could bode well for minority candidates and for teenagers from distant places.

ply early. You can boost your chances of merit money if you it your application as soon as possible. An excellent way to do s, when available, is to apply through either early action or rolling admissions.

Early action is different from early decision, which has received considerable negative press. With early decision, you apply to one school and if it sends you an acceptance letter, you're committed to attending regardless of whether it offers any financial assistance. Since this poses a huge financial gamble, it's often wealthy students who opt for early decision when applying to exclusive schools because it can increase their admission chances. In contrast, through early action you can typically apply to as many schools as you want. These acceptances are nonbinding. What's more, you won't have to commit to any of them until the standard May 1 deadline for a first-year deposit.

Applying through early action is a wonderful strategy because it lets a school know of your interest ahead of the crowd without narrowing your options. The application deadline for early action is typically between the beginning of November and the end of December. Kids who opt for early action often enjoy a greater chance of getting admitted, and they also enjoy first crack at any merit money since the pot is still full. In contrast, stragglers, who submit their applications as the regular deadline approaches, could experience problems finagling a generous package from a school.

More than 400 colleges and universities offer early action, early decision, or both. A few elite schools offer early action but require that the student approach only one institution. Make sure of an individual school's rules before applying.

Another great option is rolling admissions, which many public universities, as well as some private institutions, offer. With this approach, admissions officers make decisions about applications as they receive them. Students will often receive a verdict within one to one and a half months after submitting their paperwork. It can be easier to get into these schools if you apply early, and once again the chances of better financial assistance can be greater.

Don't fly under the radar. An increasing number of kids are showing up as stealth applicants. These are students who mystify admissions officers when their applications materialize without warning. Traditionally, students have initiated a lot of contact with admissions offices. They may request literature, visit the campus, e-mail an admissions officer, and talk to a school representative at a college fair or during a visit to the high school. Stealth applicants, however, don't do any of that. Colleges speculate that some of these applicants feel they can learn everything they need to know about a school on the Internet. Others are surely trying a scattershot approach to getting into college. They figure if they apply to enough schools, somebody is sure to bite.

This approach can bomb. One criterion that schools use when deciding whether to admit someone, much less award merit money, is whether the student has "demonstrated interest." According to a survey by the National Association for College Admission Counseling, 53% of schools are using demonstrated interest as a factor in their admission decisions. Schools worry that if they accept too many phantom applicants, who aren't serious about attending, they will have empty seats in the freshman class.

Check the right places. Not all schools award merit money. If you expect to receive a tuition break from an Ivy League school or a few elite liberal arts colleges, such as Williams, Wellesley, and Haverford colleges, which are mostly located on the East Coast, forget it. (Harvard and Yale's recent move to award large financial aid packages to upper middle class families could arguably be considered a type of merit aid.) These schools don't have to lure students with tuition discounts because they are already deluged with high quality applicants. What's more, these schools have secured a lock in the college rankings racket that is heavily biased toward old-school, old-wealth institutions.

Wealthy parents won't flinch paying full price to get into a school like Williams or Haverford, so these schools are stuffed with affluent kids paying the full freight. And between the full freight that many pay and healthy endowments, these schools can provide need-based financial aid to deserving kids, who didn't graduate from Phillips Exeter Academy, Groton School, and other private or elite suburban public high schools.

Forget the reach schools. Students like to aim for universities and colleges that they can barely squeak into. What they overlook is that these schools are not going to shower them with merit awards that they might need to make their dreams financially realistic. It's not helpful for a child to receive an acceptance letter for a school that's priced at $40,000 when the college suggests that the child and the family apply for loans. This only sets up a Catch 22 for a family. The parents will look like callous jerks if they tell their child that the school is unaffordable. But if they buckle under the pressure, they could jeopardize their own retirement by taking out a second mortgage or draining their retirement accounts to pay the tab.

Action Plan

Create demand for your child to boost his or her chances of capturing merit aid.

14

Playing the Gender Card

We have told today's young women that the world is their oyster; the problem is, so many of them believed us that the standards for admission to today's most selective colleges are stiffer for women than men. How's that for an unintended consequence of the women's liberation movement?

—Jennifer Delahunty Britz, dean of admissions and financial aid at Kenyon College

My daughter was a junior in high school when I read an op-ed piece in *The New York Times* that was written by a mother whose daughter was upset that she had been wait-listed at one of the five colleges on her list.

The essay grabbed my attention because the mother was hardly the average parent who rails against the inanity of the college admission process. The author happened to be the dean of admissions and financial aid at Kenyon College, a prestigious institution in Gambier, Ohio.

What made me panic was the mournful acknowledgement by Jennifer Delahunty Britz that admissions officers at Kenyon and many other schools are rejecting wonderfully accomplished girls simply because they are girls. And the reason? Frankly, there are just too many of them. Females now represent more than 56% of the nation's college undergraduates, and the presence of men on college campuses is expected to continue dropping.

College administrators are frightened of letting the gender divide grow too wide on their campuses. Many of them believe that the tipping point is reached when women make up 60% or more of the student body. When that happens, female applicants will sometimes look for campuses with a closer ratio of men and women. And teenage boys will cross these male-lite schools off their list because they don't want to be too outnumbered. Or at least that is the fear.

These lopsided percentages have lead to a practice that can make the parents of teenage girls shudder. Admissions offices are trying to bring the numbers back to equilibrium by giving boys a break. At the same time that schools are rejecting qualified girls, they are embracing male candidates who can thank their Y chromosomes for their admission letters. Frankly, at schools where the gender divide is reaching or is at the danger point, boys often don't have to be as qualified as the girls.

It's not tough finding schools where girls have a harder time winning over the admissions decision makers. The University of Richmond in Virginia, for instance, has manipulated the admission process so that the gender breakdown of its undergraduate population is almost identical. The University of Richmond's acceptance rate for boys was recently 43.9% versus 37.1% for girls. Swarthmore College, an elite liberal arts college in Swarthmore, Pennsylvania, recently accepted 21.2% of its male applicants, but just 15.2% of the women who applied.

It's not just private schools that are struggling with this issue. Towson University in Towson, Maryland, is one of the public schools tackling the problem. The school, where males make up just 37% of the campus population, has instituted a program that welcomes underperforming high school graduates, whose grades normally wouldn't qualify them for admission. The program primarily attracts boys.

The news for teenage girls isn't all bleak. They may enjoy a competitive advantage if they apply to schools that are overpopulated with men. These, of course, are usually the schools that are best known for their engineering programs and other technical degrees. In its latest admission figures, the Massachusetts Institute of Technology accepted 22.3% of women, but just 9.7% of men. Carnegie Mellon

University recently accepted 31.6% of its male applicants and 37.5% of the women.

What should you do, now that you know the role that gender may play in admissions? Look at gender disparities when contemplating not only your child's chances of getting into a particular school but also of his or her chances of receiving merit money or a better need-based financial aid package. A school that is desperately seeking more boys or girls could be more generous with its scholarships to those who check the right gender box on their application.

It should be easy to find out what a school's admission track record is for each sex. Just look at a school's annual Common Data Set, which is a compilation of a variety of institutional statistics that includes how many applicants of each gender apply to the school and how many are accepted. Many colleges and universities post their Common Data Set on their Web sites. A quick way to find the numbers is to Google the name of the school and "Common Data Set." You can also hunt for the data on a school's Web site or just ask the school for a copy.

Action Plan

- Teenage girls can enjoy greater success by applying to engineering schools and other institutions that attract more boys.
- Young men should consider applying to schools that have a predominance of women.

Part III

Finding Great Academic Fits

15

The Hidden Truth

When you visit a college, I don't want to say you should go and count smiles, but to some extent this whole business is more of an art than a science.

—Frederick E. Rugg, author of *Rugg's Recommendations on the Colleges, 24th Edition*

On a hot summer day in 2007, Antioch College in Yellow Springs, Ohio, announced its own obituary. The college trustees voted to close the school—at least for a few years—after the class of 2008 had graduated.

The 155-year-old college, which had been founded by abolitionists, had imploded. The once proud prominent liberal arts college, was pretty much out of money, out of students (around 300 were enrolled), and out of time.

Critiques published in *The Chronicle of Higher Education* suggested that the school's demise would hardly have been a surprise to those with any familiarity with the school. An Antioch graduate of the 1960s wrote this scathing observation in the *Chronicle*: "By the early 1990s, its once-packed library was nearly deserted. The campus itself was beyond seedy. Some buildings were crumbling, others were vandalized, and many walls were spray painted with edgy graffiti. Beer bottles and cigarette butts littered the grounds.... The library's collection was spare and dated, rich with pre-1970 books and serials, poor on materials thereafter." And esthetics and a lousy library collection were hardly the school's only problems.

Why dwell on the problems of a troubled school that will obviously not be on any teenager's list of must-see colleges in the years to come? (Since the announcement, the trustees and the alumni have been working to find ways to keep the historic college open.) Antioch can serve as a warning to any students or parents, who are tempted to rely too heavily on rankings. Here's why: Despite Antioch's severe problems, those ubiquitous college guides were still praising Antioch.

The popular *Fiske Guide to Colleges*, 2008 edition, for instance, devoted two and a half pages to Antioch in its tome that included more than "300 of the country's best and most interesting colleges and universities." *U.S. News & World Report America's Best Colleges*, 2007 edition, singled out Antioch for its high proportion of classes that contained under 20 students. It also listed Antioch in its compilation of 13 schools with "outstanding" internship programs.

The most over-the-top critique about Antioch came from a very popular book entitled *Colleges That Change Lives, 40 Schools That Will Change the Way You Think About Colleges* by Loren Pope, a former education editor at *The New York Times*. Here's what the book, which I happen to greatly admire, had to say about the school in its 2006 edition: "Antioch is in a class by itself. There is no college or university in the country that makes a more profound difference in a young person's life, or that creates more effective adults. None of the Ivies, big or small, can match Antioch's ability to produce outstanding thinkers and doers."

How could all these college experts have been so wrong about Antioch? The easy answer is that any book that tries to sum up what a particular college or university can offer by using a numerical ranking or a two-page write-up can't possibly provide a meaningful analysis of a school.

Economics explains one reason why evaluations of colleges are often superficial. Imagine spending enough time on a campus to be able to draw a realistic picture of a school's strengths and weaknesses. Now multiply that amount of time by hundreds of schools. It would require a huge commitment of man hours—and money—to compile a meaningful analysis of hundreds of schools in a guide that's cranked out annually.

That explains why a lot of the analysis is done at computer terminals far from campus quadrangles. *Fiske Guide to Colleges*, for example, obtains a great deal of background from the schools through questionnaires that it mails school administrators. Fiske also asks these administrators to distribute a different set of questionnaires to a cross section of students. What it sounds like to me is that institutions do a lot of self-grading. In other words, it doesn't sound too tough. Meanwhile, *U.S. News & World Report* relies too heavily on school reputations (deserved or undeserved) rather than trying to measure whether institutions are doing a good job of educating students.

It's fine to use these guides as a starting point. Through these books you may discover schools you didn't even know existed. You can also use them to discover what range of grade point averages and SAT or ACT scores is typically required to be admitted to a particular school. The guides can also share valuable financial aid information.

What you shouldn't do is rely heavily on these books to determine which schools you explore and which you snub. Some students believe that if a school didn't get a nod in the *Fiske* book or *Princeton Review's The Best 366 Colleges*, there must be something wrong with it. *U.S. News & World Report* induces even more snob appeal. Some kids don't want to step foot on any campus that doesn't crack the lists of the top 10 liberal art colleges and national universities.

At the same time, you shouldn't make decisions based on the marketing material that colleges generate. The promotional assault, which often starts after your child has taken the PSAT test (baby SAT) as early as his or her sophomore year, isn't just relegated to the booklets, postcards, and letters that clog mailboxes. The deft marketing is just as visible on college Web sites.

Finding and paying for the right academic fit is too important to leave to superficial snapshots of colleges and universities. There is a better alternative. In the next few chapters, you'll learn ways to evaluate schools and academic departments based on what is important to you.

Action Plan

- Don't rely on any book as the ultimate source of information on a college.
- Do your own research on colleges.

16

The Knock Against *U.S. News & World Report*

College rankings, standardized testing, costly test preparation, expensive marketing consultants for colleges, and highly-paid independent consultants for students—these and other commercial entities are profiting from fear, anxiety and myths they have helped create. As a result, college admissions have become an extravagant game to be played and education a prestigious prize to be won.

—Lloyd Thacker, founder of The Education Conservancy

Lloyd Thacker, a former admissions officer and high school counselor in Portland, Oregon, abandoned his job security a few years ago to take aim at *U.S. News & World Report*. Thacker, like many people connected to academia, considers the magazine's annual college guide harmful. The hugely popular guide, whether it intends to or not, encourages teenagers and their families to shop for schools by the numbers.

If you can finagle a spot in the freshman class of the university ranked ninth, why would you settle for a school that only occupies the twentieth spot, or the ninety-fifth spot? Or heaven forbid, why would you even bother to open the marketing material of a school that *U.S. News & World Report* relegates to the third or fourth tier?

The numbers tyranny isn't the only thing that bothers Thacker and a growing number of educators. The money-making guide has warped the way many colleges and universities attract new crops of students.

And in the process, it has changed the educational priorities of too many schools. It's this reality that has deservedly triggered increasing scorn—and even an organized revolt—that Thacker is helping to spread from ivory towers scattered across the country.

Thanks to its popularity, the magazine's annual college issue has become the equivalent of *Sports Illustrated*'s swimsuit issue and *People* magazine's sexiest man alive issue. The success also led to a pair of annual guides that can remain on newsstands throughout the year—*U.S. News & World Report America's Best Colleges* and *America's Best Graduate Schools*. According to a former managing editor, the magazine rolled out the graduate school guide because Chrysler was looking for an advertising opportunity to introduce a new vehicle.

What's Wrong with the Rankings?

For a ranking system that carries such tremendous weight, few families appreciate how the numbers are strung together. In an interview with *The Chronicle of Higher Education*, the magazine's editor called the rankings a "journalistic device" that he said is "our best judgment of what is important."

The magazine's methodology, which has been analyzed every which way by academics, clearly favors certain types of institutions. The most obvious winners are the Ivy League. One reason why Harvard, Princeton, Yale, and the other academic superstars remain insulated from competitors is because 25% of a school's ranking is based simply on its reputation—deserved or not.

Each year, the magazine sends surveys to college administrators and asks them to rank hundreds of schools based on their opinions of them. Of course, here's one of the obvious flaws in this practice: What does a college provost in Georgia or Texas know, if anything, about a school in Vermont or Minnesota and vice versa? Of course, not much. And there is nothing to stop one college from marking down another simply because it is a competitor.

The magazine's heavy reliance on the reputation of individual institutions helped fuel the outrage of a growing, but still small, number of college administrators. Thacker and the Annapolis Group, an association of leading liberal arts colleges, have been encouraging schools to refuse to fill out the annual reputation survey. And, in fact, the survey for the 2008 guide was returned by the fewest percentage of administrators ever—a mere 51%. The magazine, however, has countered that if it eventually fails to receive back a critical mass of peer assessments, it will plug the hole some other way.

The magazine's methodology favors the Ivy League and other wealthy schools even further by giving weight to the size of a school's endowment and the percentage of graduates that contribute to their alma mater. It also rewards this same elite crowd by devoting 15% of the score to student selectivity. The more kids who are rejected and the higher the test scores, the better.

An analysis by *The Chronicle of Higher Education* concluded that the ranking system seems to overwhelmingly favor private colleges and universities. Back in 1983, the first year of the rankings, eight public institutions made it onto the list of the top 25 national universities, but today only three remain. The survivors are University of California, Berkeley (21), University of Virginia (23), and UCLA (25). The schools that have made significant progress in boosting their rankings are all private.

Plenty of schools are determined to push themselves up the ladder rungs. Trustees, for instance, promised the president of Arizona State University a bonus of $10,000 if he could improve the school's ranking. Baylor University's strategic plan includes its goal of cracking the magazine's list of the top 50 national universities. *The Wall Street Journal* ran an embarrassing story about Albion College in Michigan, which was stretching the contributions of graduating seniors over five years to improve its alumni giving statistic.

One of the more controversial rankings strategies that schools have embraced is offering wealthier students merit awards. As mentioned earlier, schools historically extended academic scholarships to a small number of the brightest kids in the applicant pool. The majority of the money was reserved for middle-class and poor students who needed financial assistance. It's now common practice for schools eager to boost their rankings to offer tuition discounts to affluent students who attended college-prep high schools and achieved solid grades and SAT scores.

Here's another ploy that some schools use: They boost their applicant pool by enticing students to apply through incredibly easy online applications. Schools are eager to generate more applications so they can reject more kids and hence boost their rankings.

Many colleges and universities have been cautious about complaining because they fear being demoted in a publication that families regard as the collegiate Bible. In the mid 1990s, for instance, Reed College, a liberal arts college in Portland, Oregon, announced it would no longer cooperate with the magazine. The magazine plugged in numbers for the rebel, and Reed's rankings dropped. When Sarah Lawrence College in Bronxville, New York, stopped using the SAT, its president accused the magazine of threatening to "make up" SAT numbers for the school. The president of Drew University in Madison, New Jersey, who is a strong rankings critic, was quoted as calling the publication, "U.S. N-O-O-S-E."

An Alternative

Obviously, you need to be cautious about relying too heavily on the Cliff Notes version of academic analysis. Here's perhaps the biggest flaw in the *U.S News & World Report*'s methodology: The approach only tells you about the credentials of a school's incoming crop of freshmen. It does absolutely nothing to elucidate what kind of learning is taking place. And isn't that what finding a college should be focused on?

If you want to view the college hunt in a different light, I'd suggest buying a slim book that the crusading Thacker edited titled *College Unranked, Ending the College Admissions Frenzy*. The book, which was published by Harvard University Press, is a compilation of essays from college presidents, deans, and others in higher education who examined what's truly important when looking for the right college fit. You can order it through the Education Conservancy's Web site at www.educationconservancy.org.

Action Plan

Don't put much weight on *U.S. News & World Report*'s rankings because its methodology is greatly flawed.

17

The Rankings Antidote

An accountability process should not just "keep score," it should also help institutions improve.

—Douglas C. Bennett, president of Earlham College and chair of the National Survey of Student Engagement's National Advisory Board

Back in 1998, the Pew Charitable Trust gathered a group of higher education big shots to discuss new approaches to measuring quality on college campuses. While colleges and universities have historically had to toe the line with various accreditation bodies and jump through hoops with governmental licensing requirements, much of this involved busy work that had nothing to do with whether a child left college smarter than when he or she arrived.

Those assembled at the powwow were also concerned about the popularity of the *U.S. News & World Report* rankings, which rate schools principally on their reputations—deserved or not—as well as their exclusivity.

The meeting helped jump-start an effort that ultimately created the National Survey of Student Engagement (NSSE). The NSSE has turned into a relentless cheerleader for schools to examine how they educate their undergraduates and then do better.

While you've probably never heard of the National Survey of Student Engagement, it's worth becoming familiar with it because it peers into the yawning maw of the higher education industry and asks the sort of questions that high school kids and their parents rarely do.

The NSSE surveys more than a million students at hundreds of colleges and universities each year with the aim of measuring the richness of individual schools' learning experiences.

The NSSE, which is based at Indiana University's Center for Postsecondary Research, attempts to measure the effectiveness of a campus through its annual surveys of students in these areas:

- Academic rigor
- Active and collaborative learning
- Interactions between professors and students
- Enriching educational experiences
- Supportive campus environment

Students, for instance, are asked how often they discuss ideas and make presentations in class. How much time do students spend on homework, and how much reading and writing are assigned? Is there much contact with professors outside the classroom?

You can find the latest annual survey, as well as a list of participating schools, broken down by region, at NSSE's Web site at http://nsse.iub.edu.

Cracking the Secrecy

The annual survey discusses results only in broad terms. In one survey, for instance, freshmen at liberal arts colleges were more likely to participate in class discussions and to view their professors more positively than other institutions. In another finding, freshmen at research universities were more likely to belong to a learning community than other types of institutions.

The most recent survey concluded that students will typically boost their performance in college if they participate in at least two "high-impact" activities while in school with preferably one occurring in their freshman year. Here are those desirable activities: Belonging to a learning community, participating in undergraduate research, studying abroad, taking part in an internship, and participating in a capstone project, which usually requires seniors to use the knowledge they've gained toward earning a degree in their academic major.

Obviously, it would be helpful to know how a school fared in the yearly survey, but the NSSE doesn't release its report card of individual schools to the public. The NSSE keeps the results under wraps to encourage greater school participation because fewer of them would be willing to sign up if their dirty laundry was scattered on the campus quadrangle for all to see. It was NSSE's wish that schools on their own would voluntarily provide the report to students and families, but few had until 2007.

The secrecy started to lift when the NSSE and *USA Today* collaborated to publicize individual school results. The NSSE now encourages schools to release their benchmark scores to the newspaper.

In late 2007, the newspaper posted the latest yearly scores for 257 colleges and universities. You can examine the scores for individual schools online and compare them to the average marks for similar institutions. To access the *USA Today* scores, look for the link at the NSSE's Web site.

Hidden Gems

Even with the promise of anonymity, many schools, including those in the Ivy League, have spurned participating. It's easy to see why the Ivies, which can coast with the traditional ranking methodology, would shrink from an analysis. It's tough to do well in all five benchmarks, and many of the schools that have succeeded aren't the ones that create admission frenzies. In one year of findings, which began in 1999, these were the only schools that aced all five benchmarks:

- Beloit College, Beloit, Wisconsin
- Centre College, Danville, Kentucky
- Elon University, Elon, North Carolina
- Sweet Briar College, Sweet Briar, Virginia

The easy part, thanks to the NSSE's Web site, is finding the names of all the schools that participate in the yearly survey. Ask schools that don't release their results to *USA Today* why they don't.

Using the NSSE Survey

Even without data from an individual school, the NSSE can be helpful to students and families in a couple of ways. For starters, the annual reports include methods that some schools are using to improve the way they educate kids.

One recent report, for instance, discussed how the University of South Dakota in Vermillion, South Dakota, after spotting trends in its NSSE data, introduced a first-year experience for freshmen that included seminars and residential learning communities. The university also restructured its graduation requirements by adding an extra English course and requiring more writing in its capstone courses. In reaction to NSSE findings, Skidmore College in Saratoga Springs, New York, boosted its efforts to increase student-faculty interactions, developed a new model for its first-year experience, and strengthened its science programs.

Bennington College in Bennington, Vermont, discovered that its major challenge was cultivating a more supportive campus environment, which it set about to do. Hanover College in Hanover, Indiana, reacted to the survey by introducing a first-year experience for freshmen, revising curriculum of popular majors, and expanding the learning center. The experiences of other schools can help you formulate questions to ask at the colleges and universities that pique your interest.

Asking the Right Questions

The NSSE can also help you formulate intelligent questions when you're evaluating schools. At its Web site, you can obtain a free booklet titled *A Pocket Guide to Choosing a College, Are You Asking the Right Questions on a College Campus Visit?*

Here is a sampling of the questions:

Academic challenges

- How much time do students spend on homework each week?
- What type of thinking do assignments require?

- How much writing and reading are expected?
- To what degree are studying and spending time on academic work emphasized?

Meaningful contact with teachers

- Are faculty members accessible and supportive?
- How many students work on research projects with faculty?
- Do students receive prompt feedback on academic performance?

Active learning

- How often do students discuss ideas in class?
- How often are topics from class discussed outside or in the classroom?
- How often do students make class presentations?
- Do students work together on projects—inside and outside class?
- Additional learning opportunities
- What types of honors courses, learning communities, and other distinctive programs are offered?
- Is a culminating senior year experience required?
- How many students study in other countries?
- What percentage of students do community service?

Naming Names

The folks behind the NSSE remain steadfastly opposed to collegiate rankings. But in 2005, George D. Kuh, the organization's founder and others, published a book that names names. The book, *Student Success in College: Creating Conditions That Matter*, was the result of a 24-person research team that talked with 2,700 people during its visits to a diverse group of strong performing schools. The 20 schools enjoy higher than predicted graduation rates and, as measured by the NSSE, have successfully worked with students of differing abilities.

Here are the 20 schools that made the list:

- Alverno College, Milwaukee, Wisconsin
- California State University at Monterey Bay, Seaside, California
- Evergreen State College, Olympia, Washington
- Fayetteville State University, Fayetteville, North Carolina
- George Mason University, Fairfax, Virginia
- Gonzaga University, Spokane, Washington
- Longwood University, Farmville, Virginia
- Macalester College, St. Paul, Minnesota
- Miami University, Oxford, Ohio
- University of the South, Sewanne, Tennessee
- Sweet Briar College, Sweet Briar, Virginia
- University of Kansas, Lawrence, Kansas
- University of Maine-Farmington, Maine
- University of Michigan-Ann Arbor, Michigan
- University of Texas-El Paso, Texas
- Ursinus College, Collegeville, Pennsylvania
- Wabash College, Crawfordsville, Indiana
- Wheaton College, Norton, Massachusetts
- Winston-Salem State University, Winston-Salem, North Carolina
- Wofford College, Spartanburg, South Carolina

Action Plan

- When researching schools, use the list of questions that the National Survey for Student Engagement developed.
- Look beyond the college rankings to find incredible schools.

18

Research Made Easy

Doing research on the Web is like using a library assembled piecemeal by pack rats and vandalized nightly.

—Roger Ebert, Pulitzer Prize-winning film critic

Ever wonder where *U.S. News & World Report* and the other college guides get their statistics? You might have assumed that collecting all those figures must be incredibly labor intensive. Imagine calling hundreds or thousands of schools to ask about the average financial aid package, graduation rates, test score ranges, and many other mind-numbing figures.

Researching colleges, however, isn't nearly as hard for publishers or families as you might assume. In this chapter, you'll discover the following online resources that will make the job much easier.

The Education Trust (www.collegeresults.org)

One of my favorite higher ed resources is The Education Trust, which is a nonprofit organization that advocates for greater educational achievements among students of all ages and backgrounds. The trust's database, which is called College Results Online, provides a ton of statistics on individual schools from graduation rates to freshman retention rates to the most popular degrees granted and much more. The database also provides invaluable graduation statistics on individual schools for a variety of minority groups.

Perhaps the most amazing feature is the ability to compare the statistics of similar academic institutions. And here's the great part: You don't even have to know what schools are similar to compare and contrast them. The software does it for you. These comparisons can be quite eye opening.

To illustrate what the database can do, I randomly picked Gonzaga University in Spokane, Washington. Using the tool, I discovered that 78.4% of the students at Gonzaga, which is nationally known for its basketball team, obtain a degree in six years. That's a very respectable graduation rate; nationwide, the average six-year graduation rate for a private, nonprofit school is 63.5%. I then checked to see how successful the university was in ushering the kids out the door in four years. The graduation rate dropped to 54.8%, which was not nearly as good as many of Gonzaga's competitors.

I knew Gonzaga didn't fare as well as some of its peers because you can use the tool to compare any school to the 15, 25, or even 50 most similar institutions. For the Catholic university, Education Trust concluded that the 15 most similar schools (almost all had a religious affiliation) included Hanover College in Hanover, Indiana; Hope College in Holland, Michigan; University of Dallas (Texas); University of San Diego (California); Drake University in Des Moines, Iowa; Marquette University in Milwaukee, Wisconsin; Millsaps College in Jackson, Mississippi; and Gustavus Adolphus College in St. Peter, Minnesota.

Among these 15 peers, only the four-year graduation rates of Butler University in Indianapolis, Indiana, and University of Tulsa (Oklahoma)—54.6% and 43.2%, respectively—were worse.

In contrast, the trio of schools with the best four-year graduation rates—all above 70%—were Gustavus Adolphus, Xavier University in Cincinnati, Ohio, and Elon University in Elon, North Carolina. Gonzaga did rise back near the top of the list for five- and six-year graduation rates.

By playing with the Education Trust's tools, you can discover promising schools that you didn't know existed or become more cautious about others. Every search can generate something unexpected. For instance, when I took a look at Rhodes College, an excellent school in Memphis, Tennessee, what struck me were the statistics of other liberal arts colleges in the same cohort. The 15 liberal arts schools grouped with Rhodes included Dickinson College in Carlisle, Pennsylvania; Colorado College in Colorado Springs, Colorado; Sewanee: The University of The South in Sewanee, Tennessee; Kalamazoo (Michigan) College; and St. Olaf College in Northfield, Minnesota.

Rhodes's four-year graduation rate was very good at 77.2%, but what attracted my attention was the school at the bottom of the list—Hampshire College in Amherst, Massachusetts. The school posted the worst four-year graduation rate by a significant amount, and it also spent the least amount on its students. According to the database, Hampshire, which recently had 1,265 students enrolled, spent $15,066 per student in 2005, the most recent year of statistics. In contrast, the vast majority of its peers spent at least $21,000 per pupil. Hampshire could only muster a four-year graduation rate of 52.2%. And this is a school that recently was charging over $46,000 a year for tuition and room and board!

I encountered just as many eye openers when I looked at major research universities. Many California families will be amazed at what I discovered when I typed in the University of California, Davis, which is a highly respected research institution. UC Davis's four-year graduation rate was only 42.1%. The graduation rate of UCLA, one of Davis's sister schools, was 57%, which was better, but nothing to brag about for a university that admits only the most academically gifted students.

When reviewing the 15 most similar schools that Education Trust had grouped with UC Davis, I was fascinated to see which schools fared better. On the list, which was predominated by public universities, the University of North Carolina, Chapel Hill, topped all its competitors with a four-year graduation rate of 70.5%. The University of Michigan, Ann Arbor, came in a close second at 69.7%. Some other universities that beat out UC Davis and UCLA would stump most people, such as Miami University in Oxford, Ohio (65.5%) and the University of Delaware in Newark, Delaware (62.4%).

Of course, graduation rates are only one of innumerable measures of a school. But it's an important yardstick. Spending one or two extra years in college can not only be frustrating but also financially debilitating. Tuition and room and board at UCLA, for instance, was more than $19,000 for in-state students and more than $39,000 for outsiders clamoring to get into the school.

College Navigator (http://nces.ed.gov/collegenavigator/)

Suppose your child thinks she wants to be an occupational therapist but doesn't know what universities offer this major. Or maybe she wants to be an archaeologist or an architect or a dancer and wants to find schools either nearby or perhaps across the country.

An excellent resource to find candidates is through the federal College Navigator. The data is collected by the National Center for Education Statistics, which is within the U.S. Department of Education. The Navigator provides information on more than 7,000 two- and four-year institutions, as well as career and technical schools.

You can find schools that offer a particular major within individual states or regions, such as the Rocky Mountains, the Great Lakes, and the Southwest. When I typed "occupational therapy" into the search engine without designating any region, I got 88 hits, from Alabama State University in Montgomery, Alabama, to Xavier University in Cincinnati, Ohio. The more popular the major, the greater the number of hits. When I typed in "business" as a major, 2,344 schools appeared. In comparison, I discovered only 190 schools that provide degrees in dance.

After generating a list of candidates, you can click on any of the school links to obtain a great deal of information about the campus, including admission statistics, graduation and retention rates, financial aid information, a breakdown of the degrees of graduating seniors, and more.

U-CAN, or University & College Accountability Network www.ucan-network.org/

You can find hundreds of profiles of private colleges and universities at this relatively new site. The information compiled on all these schools is presented in a standardized form so it's very easy to navigate through the site. You can find statistics for individual schools on such things as average debt of graduating seniors, most popular degrees, freshmen retention rate, geographic and academic profile of incoming freshmen, housing options, transfer policies, study abroad opportunities, and much more. The site is the creation of the National Association of Independent Colleges and Universities, which is the largest organization representing nonprofit schools in the country.

Common Data Set

Much of the material used by college guides is extracted each year from the Common Data Set, which I've mentioned in earlier chapters. The Common Data Set was dreamed up as a way to satisfy publishers, who have a voracious appetite for higher education statistics. Schools provide figures in an annual uniform report that covers such areas as student retention and graduation rates, characteristics of the freshman class, expenses, degrees conferred by major, transfer policies, academic programs, and much more.

The statistics in a school's Common Data Set are more exhaustive than what you'll find in college guides. Many college reference books, for instance, state the percentage of students who graduate after six years, but they fail to report what percentage graduates on time. That's a frustrating omission. The data set, however, includes the number of students who graduate in four, five, and six years.

Many, but not all colleges and universities, post their Common Data Set on their Web sites for any visitor to see. Often the data is stored in a school's institutional research section. An easy way to find it is to type "Common Data Set" into a school's online search engine. Or use Google to find the form for a particular school.

If you can't locate this mother lode of data online, contact the school and ask for it.

CollegeConfidential.com

This is an online watering hole for countless students and parents who are trying to educate themselves about the college process, as well as learn more about individual schools. The site's college discussion forums, many of which focus on individual schools, generate millions of page views every month. You can post your own questions or simply read current and archived discussions. You can also send queries to a panel of college experts through the site's "Ask the Dean" section.

CollegeBoard.com

CollegeBoard.com is another resource to consult if you want to compile lists of schools that offer a particular major. The site's Match-Maker tool allows you to find schools based on your criteria, including desired majors. The tool also allows you to narrow your hunt for schools by using such factors as the type of school, location, campus life, and costs.

Wikipedia.com

When researching, it's worth checking out what Wikipedia has to say about schools that interest you. In looking for random schools on Wikipedia, I didn't come up with any institutions that weren't covered. From Illinois Institute of Technology in Chicago to Whitman College in Walla Walla, Washington, to Fordham University in New York City to Furman University in Greenville, South Carolina. Some of the coverage is more detailed and helpful than others.

The Wikipedia's write-up of Fordham University, for example, runs quite a few pages. Prospective students who research Fordham through Wikipedia will learn that all the undergraduate colleges at Fordham share a liberal arts core curriculum that consists of 17 to 21 courses drawn from nine disciplines. Teenagers reading about Whitman College will discover that roughly 50% of graduates attend graduate schools within five years.

Of course, keep in mind that Wikipedia postings are anonymous. Anyone can type in an entry or edit an existing one. Obviously, Wikipedia should only supplement your research.

Action Plan

Take advantage of free Internet tools to learn a lot about colleges in a short period of time.

19

Grading Academic Departments

One of the most common questions I am asked is, "What are the best colleges for my intended major?" I've been asked this by prospective majors in just about every subject imaginable. My reply is always the same: You are asking the wrong question. The real question students and parents should be asking at the start of their college search is not which programs are "best," but rather "What are the elements of a strong program in a particular major?"

—Carolyn Z. Lawrence, private college counselor and founder of AdmissionsAdvice.com

Not long ago, the new dean of the nationally renowned journalism school at Northwestern University received free reign to overhaul the place. To pave the way for changes, the university's administrators temporarily suspended faculty governance in the journalism school. With newspapers threatening to become as relevant as a wooly mammoth, the university's goal in instigating the makeover was to bring the teaching of the next generation of journalism students into the twenty-first century.

No longer would a student reporter who was heading for an assignment leave with just a pen and a notebook. These would-be multimedia journalists would be routinely equipped with such equipment as digital camcorders and video iPods. What's more, the revamped curriculum would require students to become familiar with marketing techniques.

Critics view the new emphasis on selling the news and online journalism as practically sacrilegious. Journalists who want to pursue careers in the traditional print media, they insist, shouldn't have to worry about marketing, editing tape, or blogging.

What does this academic dustup have to do with evaluating an academic department? Even if your child has no intention of becoming a journalist, the imbroglio at Northwestern is worth noting because it illustrates the importance of not making assumptions about any department or school simply based on a college or university's reputation.

With or without the reforms, Northwestern is considered one of the best journalism schools in the country, and its competitors are watching Northwestern's trailblazing experiment. But if a student is dead set on immersing him- or herself in classic print journalism, Northwestern may or may not be the best bet. On the other hand, if a child is intrigued by new journalism approaches, a school with a more traditional curriculum might not fit.

With every student's talents, needs, and career goals so different, it's important to learn as much as you can about the academic department or the school within a university where you will be spending a lot of your time.

The worst way to evaluate an academic department is to simply rely on the reputation of the college or university. Plenty of parents and kids assume that any institution with platinum credentials is going to be bursting with excellent programs in every department. Attending a university with a nationally renowned journalism school, however, doesn't guarantee that the professors who teach in the psychology or philosophy department are going to be stellar.

On the flip side, you shouldn't assume that a college that hasn't endeared itself to the ranking meisters at *U.S. News & World Report* isn't blessed with academic departments bursting with smart, innovative teachers, who are dedicated to their students.

Research Nuts and Bolts

How do you evaluate departments? Consider approaching the task as if you were researching a term paper. The more sources you use, the better. Once you've immersed yourself in the issues that involve teaching a particular major, whether it's biology, sociology, or occupational therapy, the better able you'll be to tell what's important and what's just fluff when you focus on departments of particular schools.

Individual schools shouldn't be your only source of information about majors. After all, they will almost certainly insist they are academically superior. In this chapter, then, you'll find outside sources to help you ultimately do a bang-up job of learning how different majors are taught and evaluating academic departments. In Chapter 20, "Grading Academic Departments, Part II," you learn how to evaluate individual programs after you've narrowed down the field of schools.

Here are some resources to use:

Read the trades. You can learn an amazing amount about the art of teaching college students—in just about any imaginable field—by peeking over the shoulders of journalists who cover higher education for an academic audience. Two excellent resources are *The Chronicle of Higher Education* and *Inside Higher Ed*.

Inside Higher Ed (www.insidehighered.com) is a free online publication, launched in 2004 that provides daily news and commentary about academia. The better known *Chronicle* (www.chronicle.com), which bills itself as the No. 1 source of news and jobs for the industry, publishes a print and online edition, but neither is free. You can purchase a week Web pass for $11.95 and subscriptions start at $40 for six months. Both publications archive their stories, which will make any search easier.

What can you learn from these news sources to justify spending time hunched over your computer? Here is just one example of what you can stumble across with very little effort: I typed "innovative" and "sciences" into *Inside Higher Ed*'s search engine to see what I'd find. One of the articles that popped up was "Best Practices in Undergrad

Research." The article described a book that the Council on Undergraduate Research had just released that highlights innovative research strategies at individual schools. The article also mentioned big trends in the scientific disciplines. Cutting-edge science departments are developing interdisciplinary approaches to instruction, as well as embracing inquiry-based labs where students generate questions. Creative professors are also trying to shake the lonely scientist stereotype by emphasizing teamwork in classrooms.

The *Chronicle* covered similar ground in a lengthy piece that explored ways that professors are energizing notoriously impersonal introductory science classes. These intro classes tend to wash out a lot of kids. By one estimate, about 30% of freshmen expect to earn a bachelor's degrees in science, math, or engineering, but only 15% graduate in those fields.

It's simple to use these publications with their myriad of links to their own archives and to outside organizations as a cheap or free research assistant no matter what education topic you want to research.

Check out professional organizations. You can learn a lot about a major, the institutions that offer it, innovative teaching approaches, and potential careers by eavesdropping on what professionals and/or educators in a particular field are saying. Some professional organizations actually go out of their way to include students or prospective students in their fields.

One of the nice things about many of these professional groups is the low cost. In many cases, an investment of just $20 or $30 will buy you a year's worth of professional publications, as well as access to the group's Web site.

A student, for example, can join the American Society for Engineering Educators for a mere $20 a year. In return, a student member receives a magazine that includes articles about educators and creative engineering programs, as well as the opportunity to obtain an annual publication called *Profiles of Engineering & Engineering Technology Colleges*, which profiles engineering programs in this country and Canada. Members also receive free online access to the quarterly *Journal of Engineering Education*, which normally costs $150, as well as a regular online engineering news briefing called *First Bell*. And student members get to attend the society's annual conference for free.

Thanks to Google, it shouldn't be tough finding professional organizations tied to your student's possible major.

Student organizations. There are also organizations devoted to students or prospective students in particular fields. A great place for wannabe architects, for example, is ARCHcareers.org, which is connected to the American Institute of Architecture Students (AIAS) and the American Institute of Architects. The site is dedicated to helping high school students and undergraduates who want to study architecture. If you still have questions after visiting, you can post them to the site's Dr. Architecture.

To help evaluate these schools, AIAS has posted on its Web site at www.aias.org a list of questions to pose to faculty at prospective architecture schools. You will learn far more if you subscribe to *Crit*, the AIAS's twice-yearly journal, which covers current issues in architectural education and the profession.

Don't assume a major can't be cutting edge. You might think that certain majors couldn't possibly be confronted with the sort of dramatic teaching changes that journalism schools or science departments are contemplating—much less the frequent technological advances that engineering departments must grapple with. But that's not true. Any major can benefit from innovation and change.

Foreign language provides an excellent example of this phenomenon. As with some other humanities departments, language teachers have been instructing students pretty much the same way for many decades—and probably much longer.

Traditionally, students have mastered a language's vocabulary and grammar rules and then they devote the rest of their time taking advanced literature classes in the foreign language. The Modern Language Association, which is the professional organization for language teachers, now insists, however, that this age-old way of teaching is antiquated. Writing brilliant papers in French on *Madame Bovary*, *Candide*, and other famous French novels isn't necessarily going to prepare you for jobs that require bilingual skills. Consequently, language departments are now being urged to introduce curriculums that can better prepare students for a global society. That means bringing in other disciplines that can better help them use their language proficiency in a variety of careers.

Since many of the professors in language departments are literature professors, the changes that the Modern Language Association are pushing, aren't being warmly greeted at many institutions. Learning about this new wrinkle in language education, however, can help you formulate more intelligent questions for department faculty. And language students will need to ask themselves whether they want to learn the old-fashioned way.

One of the best ways to keep up with developments in language education is to join the Modern Language Association (www.mla.org). The new membership rate is $35, and that includes a subscription to MLA publications that feature essays on undergraduate and graduate curriculum and approaches to teaching.

Check accreditation. Another place to research is at the Web sites of accrediting agencies. Not all academic majors fall under the umbrella of outside accreditors, but plenty do.

You can start your search at the online home of the Council for Higher Education Accreditation (www.chea.org), which is an organization of 3,000 colleges and universities. The council recognizes 60 accreditation programs for degrees ranging from landscape architecture and interior design to occupational therapy and library science.

Prowling at an accrediting organization's Web site can be helpful for a couple of reasons. It's an easy way to learn which schools offer programs that have been accredited in particular majors. It takes a lot of work to successfully survive an accreditation process, so it's useful to see what institutions have earned this seal of approval.

Recently 460 business schools and departments, for example, received a nod from the Association to Advance Collegiate Schools of Business (AACSB), but that pales compared to the roughly 2,400 schools that offer business. Does that mean the rest are inferior? Absolutely not.

In fact, schools sometimes chafe at accreditation mandates. For instance, the requirements dictated by ABET, Inc. (formerly known as Accreditation Board for Engineering and Technology) were criticized in the past for being too rigid. Some critics suggested that the accreditors were more interested in the quantity of classes rather than the teaching quality and the ultimate educational results. Changes in the engineering requirements, however, now allow engineering schools more latitude in developing their own programs.

Accreditors, though, can provide an idea of what a premiere program in a student's field may look like. Some of the accreditation organizations, such as the AACSB, post their standards on their Web sites. You may also find other materials worth reading. For instance, AACSB posts current and archived issues of *BizEd*, which explores the latest trends in business education, on its Web site. In one issue, for example, an article explored how computer simulations are helping students learn more about global business challenges, and another talked about business schools that have launched microfinance initiatives to teach students about pressing global issues.

You'll find all the accrediting agencies that have received the imprimatur of the Council for Higher Education Accreditation at its Web site, www.chea.org/Directories/special.asp.

Here's a sampling of various accreditation programs:

- **Architecture—**National Architectural Accrediting Board (www.naab.org)
- **Business—**Association to Advance Collegiate Schools of Business (www.aacsb.edu)
- **Education—**National Council for Accreditation of Teacher Education (www.ncate.org); Teacher Education Accreditation Council (www.teac.org)
- **Engineering—**ABET, Inc., formerly Accreditation Board for Engineering and Technology (www.abet.org)
- **Fine Arts—**National Association of Schools of Dance (http://nasd.arts-accredit.org); National Association of Schools of Music (http://nasm.arts-accredit.org); National Association of Schools of Art and Design (http://nasad.arts-accredit.org/); National Association of Schools of Theater (http://nast.arts-accredit.org)
- **Journalism—**Accrediting Council on Education in Journalism and Mass Communications (www2.ku.edu/~acejmc)
- **Nursing—**Commission on Collegiate Nursing Education (www.aacn.nche.edu/accreditation)

- **Pharmacy—**Accreditation Council for Pharmacy Education (www.acpe-accredit.org)
- **Physical Therapy—**American Physical Therapy Association (www.apteonline.org)
- **Psychology—**American Psychological Association (www.apa.org)
- **Social Work—**Council on Social Work Education (www.cswe.org)

Another resource to check is the U.S. Department of Education's Database of Accredited Postsecondary Institutions and Programs at http://ope.ed.gov/accreditation/.

Action Plan

Learn as much about your potential major as possible before you start shopping for colleges.

20

Grading Academic Departments, Part II

There are standout programs at some average institutions and some terrible programs at well-regarded institutions. Global evaluations of an institution's "reputation" do students a disservice when they take the place of getting facts about the program in which the student wishes to enroll.

—Comment posted on *The Chronicle of Higher Education*'s news blog

When Carl E. Wieman, a fixture in the physics department at the University of Colorado at Boulder, won the Nobel Prize in Physics in 2001, you might have expected him to soak up the accolades and continue his impressive research.

But what really excited the physicist was a much trickier challenge: improving the way college-level science is taught. He was particularly keen on improving the lot of students who get crammed into impersonal introductory science courses, where rote memorization is rewarded, and monstrous class sizes are routine.

When Nobel Prize winners speak, college administrators listen, and what Wieman requested from the University of Colorado was a financial commitment to improve its science teaching methods. When university administrators became distracted by scandals involving its football team and a controversial professor, Wieman told *The Chronicle of Higher Education* that he decided to move to the University of British Columbia, which promised to bankroll a science education initiative that is named after him.

The experience of the physicist, who was later named the 2004 U.S. Professor of the Year among all doctoral and research universities, illustrates just how difficult it can be to change ingrained academic behavior. If a Nobel Prize winner can't instigate an academic revolution at a school, it's hard to imagine who can. (The University of Colorado did end up launching a more modest science education effort and is paying its former Nobel Prize winner to advise it.) An increasing number of professors at colleges and universities, however, are experimenting with innovative ways of teaching.

An eagerness to innovate is one of the hallmarks of a top-notch academic department that you should be looking for as you research how particular majors are taught at individual schools. In Chapter 19, "Grading Academic Departments," you learned some of the ways you can familiarize yourself with how disciplines are generally taught as well as educational trends. Armed with that knowledge, you'll learn ways to evaluate a major offered on a particular campus.

Here's are what you need to do:

Read the press coverage. You can get a quick idea whether the department has won accolades or has done anything to merit media attention by looking at press releases generated by a college or university's in-house writers. If the institution publishes an alumni magazine, look in its archive. But don't stop at what you find from these sources, which are obviously self-serving. Use the college Web site to find campus newspaper coverage not only on a particular department but about life at this school—warts and all. Check the online archives of the local paper to find coverage of academic programs. Also peruse the educational trade journals mentioned in Chapter 19—*The Chronicle of Higher Education* (www.chronicle.com) and *Inside Higher Ed* (www.insidehighered.com). And don't forget Google.

Look for creativity. Plenty of professors get stuck in a rut. They teach the same way, year in and year out as their material becomes drier than burnt toast. Some of these educators would rather cling to the familiar than explore new approaches.

This pigheadedness is what educators who participated in an online discussion hosted by *The Chronicle of Higher Education* grumbled about one morning. The professors, scattered around the country, had gathered on the Web to hear the thoughts of Robert J.

Beichner, a physics professor at North Carolina State University in Raleigh. Beichner has received many positive strokes for developing a promising way to banish impersonal lectures for science and engineering students. Schools throughout the country, including the Massachusetts Institute of Technology, have adopted the teaching approach.

In talking about the academic resistance to change, Beichner shared his take on the phenomenon: "It's probably true that nearly all higher education faculty members were very good students in the traditional classroom setting. This leads to inertia. 'It was good enough for me, so it's good enough for them.' So many introductory course become filters instead of pumps. What ends up happening is that people who think as we do will succeed and the rest won't. But we can no longer afford to only concentrate ourselves with 2% or 3% of our students."

Creative teaching approaches are especially important during a student's early semesters because that's when they are likely to wash out. Large impersonal lecture classes can prompt students to lose interest or abandon grueling majors.

There is no one great source to find out about innovative teaching. If a department is thinking outside the box, it will probably tout its efforts on its Web site. When you contact professors by e-mail or during a campus visit, ask about teaching approaches.

Check department Web sites. The online home of academic departments should provide a more unfiltered look at what kind of learning is going on compared to the marketing propaganda that admissions offices crank out.

The departmental site should include the academic credentials of all the faculty, as well as the research they've conducted and a description of its courses and their schedules. The site should also tell you whether a senior thesis or capstone project is required, the department encourages internships, helps with scholarship opportunities, and provides tutoring. Also check to see whether professors collaborate with undergraduates in research projects, which are growing in popularity. And note any description of a department's research facilities.

Ultimately, what you'd like to see is a department that has plenty to brag about. The physics department at North Carolina State

University in Raleigh, for example, is not shy about touting its accomplishments. The department is the ninth largest in the country (out of 751) and has more women on the faculty than any other in the nation. Its ability to attract research money places it in the top three departments on its campus and in the top 25 of physics departments in the country. When it surveyed its students in the last school year, 90% expressed satisfaction with the teaching.

The physics faculty has also won a slew of outstanding teaching awards and, as mentioned earlier, the department has instituted an innovative way of teaching introductory courses that has spread elsewhere. The department also posted its 36-page strategic plan that is stuffed with goals. In addition, the site mentions that its research opportunities are for graduate and undergraduate students. It's hard not to be impressed when you see a department display this kind enthusiasm, drive, and achievement.

Find out who is teaching. The academic headliners who bring fame to a department are often not the ones who teach. That's because professors at research universities, in particular, aren't rewarded for teaching undergraduates. They garner brownie points by publishing papers and attracting grants. For too many university professors, teaching undergraduates is a nuisance with office hours barely tolerated.

Consequently, you should look at the school's academic catalogue and department Web sites to determine who is teaching what. Are the most respected professors teaching undergraduates? Or is this task shoved off on adjunct professors, academic fellows, and others who are still trying to make a name for themselves?

Check the numbers. Statistics can be misleading. And a big whopper is often the student-to-faculty ratio, which you'll find in many college guides. To get that figure, schools divide the number of faculty versus the student body. But what about professors perched high in the food chain who teach graduate students and rarely bother with undergraduates? Those professors still get thrown into the equation.

For a more realistic alternative, ask about the average class size of courses at the school as well as in introductory classes and those in your major.

Weigh a major's popularity. You should also be curious about how many students graduate from a school with a particular major. It's easy to find this out at the federal College Navigator (http://nces.ed.gov/collegenavigator), which I mentioned in a previous chapter. A critical mass of majors can bring more faculty and greater resources.

For an example, I used the online locator to see the departmental breakdown of recent graduates at Lehigh University in Bethlehem, Pennsylvania, which is known for its engineering and business schools. Sure enough, the school's most popular degrees in a recent year were in engineering (292) and business (320). In contrast, three students graduated with degrees in environmental science.

On the flip side, kids choosing popular majors want to make sure that they won't get stymied when they try enrolling in classes. What's crept into the lexicon of higher ed is the term "impacted major," which is shorthand for this reality: "If you think you're going to graduate in four years, you're nuts!" With a crush of students all requiring the same courses—which may only be taught once a year—students can find it hard to graduate in four or even five years.

Check graduation track records. Before enrolling in a school, find out its four-year graduation rate. Also ask how long it typically takes students with a particular major to graduate. In addition, find out whether pursuing a double major would slow down your pursuit of a degree.

Many college guides provide only six-year graduation rates, but do you know any parents who would shrug off being forced to pay tens of thousands of dollars more because their children were shut out of the classes they needed for a speedy graduation? Schools that initially appear cheap won't necessarily be a bargain when students must delay the start of their careers through no fault of their own. You can discover how to pinpoint graduation rates in Chapter 18, "Research Made Easy."

Contact professors. You can get an idea of how receptive teachers are to students by e-mailing them. Your questions should show that you've spent time researching the department. If your e-mails are ignored, you may naturally wonder how the teachers would treat you as a student.

Before visiting a school, try to arrange to meet with one or two faculty in your major. After sessions with professors, you might get a better sense of whether you'd feel comfortable in their classrooms.

That's what the son of a good friend of mine did when he toured a private university in New York State. The university enjoyed a great reputation for its music program, but when the future music major met with the professor he would be spending the most time with, he eliminated the school from his list. While the school offered the budding jazz guitarist a scholarship, he didn't feel comfortable with the professor, and ultimately ended up at Temple University in Philadelphia.

Ask students. If you visit a campus, consider attending a class in your expected major. Before or after the class, ask students what they think of the teachers and the program.

Think ahead. If you believe you'll eventually want to earn a master's or professional degree, explore what these graduate programs want. Visit the Web sites of departments and schools within universities to see what kind of academic background they expect from their graduate students. Compare that with what schools on your list offer. Some of the questions you should pose are: What do students who receive this degree do after graduation? How many go into graduate school, and what is the acceptance rate of those who apply from this institution and department? How many get jobs right away?

Action Plan

- Never assume that an academic department is solid just because the school's overall reputation is sterling.
- Use press coverage, a department's own Web site, and easy-to-access online resources when evaluating an academic discipline within a school.

21

The Value of Undergraduate Research

I found myself more motivated to do course work while doing research, because I finally saw the application of what I've been learning. At the same time, being constantly around principal investigators, post-docs, and graduate students can be very humbling—it makes you realize how truly little you know about things.

—Erika Ilagan, undergraduate biochemistry major at University of Rochester; her research project: "Biochemical Properties of Simian Immunodeficiency Virus (African Green Monkey) Reverse Transcriptase Variants"

In 2007, a food science professor at Clemson University made national headlines for debunking a belief that mothers of toddlers and millions of other Americans have held for years: If you drop your peanut butter sandwich, a pacifier, or anything else, you can still safely stick it back in your mouth if you pick it up quickly. The researchers, however, concluded that even five seconds leaves plenty of time for bacteria to hop on a sandwich.

The reason for mentioning this research isn't to make you feel guilty next time you eat something off the floor. What makes this research notable is that the idea for the study, as well as much of the footwork, came from undergraduates.

The students were participating in one of Clemson University's Creative Inquiry groups. The Creative Inquiry program allows a small group of students to typically spend three or four semesters pursuing a research project under the guidance of one professor. The research groups have been expanding rapidly on the campus, and the South Carolina school hopes to ultimately involve all of its undergraduates—that's nearly 14,200 kids—in the program.

Unfortunately, the experiences that Clemson students enjoy are not nearly common enough among undergraduates elsewhere. It's the graduate students who have traditionally been encouraged to conduct research. Studies, however, show that all students can greatly benefit from working on research projects with their professors. Consequently, when evaluating academic departments, it makes sense to learn whether they offer undergraduate research opportunities.

In fact, one way students can increase their chance of success at college is to participate in undergraduate research. The National Survey of Student Engagement, a highly regarded organization that measures the quality of student learning, has concluded that research by undergraduates is one of a handful of "high impact" practices that boost student performance inside and outside the classroom. The Association of American Colleges and Universities also singled out undergraduate research as one of the more promising practices that a school can provide its students.

The benefits of undergraduate research are many. Conducting research at a young age can develop critical thinking, problem solving, and greater self confidence. Students can also benefit by working closely with a faculty mentor. Undergraduate research opportunities can be even more welcome at large schools, where students, particularly in their freshman and sophomore years, may spend significant time in lecture halls.

Research projects can also shrink the number of casualties in the fields of science, technology, engineering, and math. The crush of students who bail from these majors is troubling. What's more, introducing students to the world of academic research may propel more of them into graduate schools or better prepare them for a career.

Students shouldn't assume that research is an option only for science and engineering geeks. Students pursuing any major, from entomology to art history, could appreciate the chance to become junior researchers.

The University of Delaware is one of the rarer animals that provides research opportunities not only to students in sciences and engineering but to humanities majors as well. Nearly all of Delaware's faculty collaborate with student researchers in engineering and sciences, but what's more surprising is that about two-thirds of the faculty in the humanities regularly work with undergraduates in their research. In fact, some students have chosen the Delaware flagship because they are eager to participate in research projects with professors in such classic humanities majors as literature, foreign languages, and philosophy.

When investigating schools, be sure to check out research opportunities. An easy way to get started is to type "undergraduate research" into a school's search engine. You'll discover that some institutions have dropped the ball, while others are devoting considerable resources to the effort.

The University of Rochester, an upstate New York school, for instance, institutionalized its research commitment by creating an Office of Undergraduate Research and Mentoring. It also offers students a chance to publish their work through *The Journal of Undergraduate Research*. At Carnegie Mellon University, undergrads can apply for grants of up to $1,000 for research projects in all fields of study, and the university sponsors a yearly symposium where undergrads share their research.

When visiting a campus ask about research opportunities not only campuswide but also in individual departments. Also check the Web sites of academic departments, which may help you gauge their commitment to introducing students to meaningful research.

You can learn more about the value of undergraduate research by visiting the Web site of the Council On Undergraduate Research (www.cur.org), which was started 30 years ago by a group of chemists who taught at liberal arts colleges. Another resource is the Web Guide to Research for Undergraduates (WebGURU), based at Northeastern University, which is aimed at helping undergrads navigate research hurdles (www.webguru.neu.edu).

Action Plan

Look for schools that provide research opportunities to undergraduates.

22

Grading Professors

His lectures are like reading Charles Dickens; long, boring, and never ending.

I swear, she must have gotten her degree out of a vending machine.

If you are entertained by strange old men, he's a keeper!

—Comments posted on ProfessorPerformance.com

James D. Miller, an associate economics professor at Smith College in Northampton, Massachusetts, thinks he's figured out a way to get his peers to do a better job of teaching: Bribe them.

Here's his idea: Schools would give each graduating senior $1,000 to reward the professors they valued the most. Miller argued that students would take the task more seriously than they would end-of-the-semester evaluations. Colleges that embraced the reward system could end up attracting many more star teachers. What's more, with students dangling $1,000 carrots, professors might think twice before blowing off their office hours or sleepwalking through their lectures.

Or at least that's the hope. Unfortunately, we'll never know whether this idea would work since it's unlikely that schools will embrace it. In lieu of those cash prizes, students are grading individual professors at online collegiate watering holes.

A variety of Web sites are encouraging students to share their feelings about their teachers so that others will be better able to avoid the skunks and find the gems. The idea makes sense. When students plow through course catalogues, they are often clueless about the teachers who they will be stuck with for several months. Are these teachers going to be duds or inspirational?

Here are three Web sites that let students do the grading:

RateMyProfessors.com. This site posts student ratings on professors teaching at more than 6,000 schools in the United States, Canada, and Great Britain. Thousands of new ratings are added every day. When I logged on, the most popular teachers, highlighted on its home page, included a health science professor at Indiana University, a journalism teacher at the University of Minnesota, and a science teacher at Ocean County College in Toms River, New Jersey. Students use a numerical scale to evaluate. It also lets kids vote on whether a teacher is "hot."

PickaProf.com. In addition to student comments, visitors can ostensibly see who are the hard graders at a school and who are pushovers. PickaProf receives grade distributions on individual classes, as well as drop rates.

ProfessorPerformance.com. This site offers students a chance to grade their professors, as well as type in their own written evaluations. You can search the A+ Club, which showcases professors at individual schools who have scored an average grade of B+ or higher.

The Value of Online Ratings

Is it worth it to check out these academic popularity sites? A couple of researchers at Marist College in Poughkeepsie, New York, attempted to answer that question in a study titled "He Will Crush You Like an Academic Ninja!": Exploring Teacher Ratings on RateMyProfessors.com. In their own words, here's what the researchers concluded:

> The present research revealed that student postings on the website RateMyProfessors.com closely matched students' real life concerns about the quality of instruction in the classroom. While issues such as personality and appearance did enter into the postings, these were secondary motivators compared to more salient issues such as competence, knowledge, clarity, and helpfulness. Students post comments as a way to

> both receive and share information about instructors. They value the perspective of their peers, but are also critical consumers of the posted comments.

In other words, it sounds like the web sites are worth checking out.

Action Plan

Check out what students are saying about professors at individual schools.

Part IV

Overlooked Academic Choices

23

Stop Hyperventilating

> *As Ivy League universities report—once again—that admissions rates have fallen to record lows, newspapers rush to publish stories documenting the increasingly "frenzied" (variants: "frantic," "brutal") competition among students vying for a coveted slot in an elite school.... There's just one problem: It's not true. The declining odds of getting into an elite college are mostly a statistical mirage, caused by confusion between college applicants and college applications.*
>
> —Kevin Carey, research and policy manager at Education Sector

Every spring, students and parents gasp when they read about the latest student casualties in the college admissions arms race. Each year, has seemed more difficult to get into colleges and universities as the number of high school graduates continued to mushroom. There seems to be bountiful statistics to support this phenomenon that has triggered so many panic attacks.

Recently, for instance, only 9% of applicants managed to charm their way into Yale University, while three years earlier 11% received fat acceptance packages. During the same time period, acceptances dropped from 16% of applicants to 13% at the Massachusetts Institute of Technology and from 13% to 11% at Stanford. In illustrating just how ridiculously impossible it is to impress the admissions gods, journalists invariably find an Ivy reject who is a student body president/valedictorian with perfect SAT scores and is on the verge of discovering a cure for some horrible disease.

Reading these annual dispatches is enough to make any parents think that their children need to be darn near perfect to have any chance of spending four years at a first-rate school. But that's nonsense. In UCLA's latest annual survey of college freshmen across the country, more than 67% of students were attending their first choice school. So for the vast majority of high school seniors, creeping exclusivity is not an issue.

Even those who regrettably believe that their young lives would end if they can't attend one of the most selective schools on the planet shouldn't be discouraged. In reality, the academic bar isn't being raised as much as the media dispatches insist. The source of this happy news bulletin is the Education Sector, which is a nonprofit education policy think tank.

In examining admission statistics, Education Sector acknowledged that the number of high schools graduates banging on college doors has been increasing. But here's the comforting part: The most competitive schools are accepting more students. The Ivy League schools, for instance, increased the number of acceptances they extended by almost 11% between 2002 and 2006, which was greater than the growth of high school seniors. Education Sector also looked at roughly 60 institutions considered "most competitive" by *Barron's Guide to Colleges* and noticed the same trend. These schools accepted 199,821 student in 2002, but the number jumped by 8% to 215,738 four years later.

The increase in acceptances among select schools has been overlooked because of the media's fixation on applications rather than applicants. The acceptance statistics look worse because they are dependent on the number of applications that schools receive not the number of applicants, which is dramatically lower. Suppose that a student applies to five schools and gets into three. If he applies to 15 schools instead and gets into three, the result for this child is the same. He earned an acceptance into three schools. But all the applications he sent in made the competition look worse than it actually is.

One reason for the application creep has been the growing number of high school graduates. In addition, more kids are applying to more schools. In the 1960s, less than 2% of high schoolers applied to six or more colleges, but today more than 2% are applying to at least 11 schools.

Another culprit is the number of students applying to more competitive schools. Kevin Carey, the Education Sector's research and policy manager, suggests that more kids who have no chance of getting in are knocking on the doors of the nation's most select schools. "There has likely been an increase in the number of unqualified students treating the Harvard application like a Powerball ticket," Carey wrote in an article in *The American Prospect*. "An Ivy League education can be worth millions of dollars over a lifetime. To take a shot at one, all you need is $65 and a dream."

Action Plan

Stay calm. The vast majority of students get accepted by their No. 1 academic choice.

24

The Allure of Liberal Arts Colleges

Families believe that if their teenagers don't attend highly selective, name-brand colleges, they won't be successful. It reminds me of Groucho Marx's quote, "I don't want to belong to any club that will accept me as a member," but this is not based in reality at all.

—Martha "Marty" O'Connell, executive director, Colleges That Change Lives

My daughter was in middle school when she started talking about colleges. One night at dinner, she told my husband and me that she wanted to attend the University of California, Berkeley, or maybe UCLA.

We knew why she focused on these state schools. Her friends were talking about them. We happen to live in California, where, according to *The Chronicle of Higher Education*, 84% of students end up at state institutions. It's only natural then that teenagers and their parents initially focus on the most prestigious of the bunch.

Californians aren't any different from families in much of the rest of the country. For most teenagers, public schools are the obvious choice. In Texas, 87% of college students attend public institutions. The numbers are also high in the state of Washington (85%), Michigan (80%), Louisiana (92%), Virginia (80%), New Mexico (92%), and frankly just about every other state except a few that are huddled primarily in the Northeast.

We figured Caitlin would end up at a large state school, but that was before someone suggested reading a book entitled *Colleges That Change Lives: 40 Schools That Will Change the Way You Think About Colleges*, by Loren Pope, a former education editor of *The New York Times*. Pope eventually became an independent college counselor and an unabashed and tireless supporter of liberal arts colleges.

Frankly, it had never occurred to my daughter or me to look at small colleges, but after reading Pope's book we were curious. Ultimately we visited 12 liberal arts colleges located in the Pacific Northwest and on the East Coast, as well as a handful of universities. We discovered some lovely liberal arts schools, such as Muhlenberg College in Allentown, Pennsylvania; University of Puget Sound in Tacoma, Washington; Willamette University in Salem, Oregon; Franklin & Marshall College in Lancaster, Pennsylvania; Ursinus College in Collegeville, Pennsylvania; Reed College in Portland, Oregon; Skidmore College in Saratoga Springs, New York; Goucher College in Baltimore, Maryland; and Whitman College in Walla Walla, Washington.

After our travels, my daughter's desire to share a school with tens of thousands of classmates evaporated. In fact, by the time she was a senior in high school, she had zero interest in attending any state school in California. Before we let her bail on the cheaper state universities, however, we told her that she had to earn a merit award to defray the extra cost of any private college she selected. And she did. Five of the eight schools where she applied kicked in cash, and she narrowed her final list down to Juniata College and Dickinson College, which are located 84 miles away from each other in central Pennsylvania. She is currently a happy camper at Juniata.

Of course, liberal arts schools aren't for everybody. It won't be a fit for the teenager who would become claustrophobic attending a school with just 1,000 to 2,000 students. It won't be a suitable choice for many kids, who expect to major in fields beyond the liberal arts sphere of the sciences, math, psychology, English, history, fine arts, and other humanities. Only a tiny number of liberal arts colleges, for instance, offer engineering degrees. And these intimate academic outposts might not be satisfactory for students eager to see their school compete in a bowl game or during March Madness.

Even after eliminating all these square pegs, however, plenty of students remain who could become captivated by small schools if they bothered to look. And here are reasons why:

Small classes. At liberal arts colleges, you're not going to get stuck in a lecture hall that requires TV monitors to see the professor, who is hugging the lectern. A few large introductory courses might contain 40 or 50 kids, but many classes contain two dozen students or less. When touring Willamette University, for instance, the tour guide proudly showed us the largest classroom on the campus—it held only 35 kids. In my daughter's first semester at Juniata, her conversational Spanish professor thought too many kids had enrolled in the class. The original class contained just 16 students! He split the class in half and taught back-to-back sessions just so his students could get more time speaking Spanish.

Student focused. The rap against universities is that too many professors are more interested in their research than their students. This phenomenon is understandable because universities don't reward professors for their teaching prowess. Pulling in research grants and publishing in peer-reviewed journals are what helps win tenure. With professors occupied with their own projects, teaching assistants are often relied on to grade papers and even teach classes. Another huge focus for professors at research institutions is grooming their graduate students.

At liberal arts colleges, professors aren't distracted by graduate students' needs because there usually aren't any. The primary focus of teachers on these campuses is teaching undergraduates, and research comes second.

Preparation for graduate school. At small schools, there are often more chances for students to work directly with professors in research projects. What's more, assignments can be more meaningful. Professors, for instance, would be more inclined to assign a paper on the symbolism in a Franz Kafka novel if they had to grade only 20 papers rather than 500. In fact, some liberal arts colleges pride themselves on the writing-intensive nature of their classes. With fewer students, professors can be less likely to rely heavily on impersonal lectures that lead to rote learning and a lot of multiple choice tests.

The rigor of the curriculum and the extra attention can more than prepare students for graduate or professional schools.

It's a fallacy that you've got a better chance of getting into grad school if you attend a state research institution as a undergraduate. In fact, on a per capita basis, liberal arts colleges produce twice as many students who earn a PhD in science than other institutions. What's more, small schools dominate the list of the top 10 institutions that produce the most students who ultimately earn doctorate degrees.

Endless examples exist that illustrate how liberal arts schools serve as staging grounds for graduate educations. Reed College, for instance, ranks in the top three of all U.S. colleges and universities for the percentage of graduates who earn PhD's in all fields. Pomona College in Claremont, California, sent a higher percentage of its graduates to Harvard Law School during a recent year than Brown or Duke universities. A higher percentage of students at Grinnell College in Iowa receive PhD's than Harvard and Yale alumni. Graduates at my daughter's college enjoy a 95% acceptance rate at all postgraduate programs including medicine, dental, and law schools.

Cost. On the surface, private schools are more expensive. But, as mentioned elsewhere in the book, sticker prices are often a joke. Unlike many public universities, plenty of private schools have deeper institutional pockets to hand out cash. If a private school covets your child, it can make a generous offer. In fact, thanks to financial aid grants and/or merit awards, it's possible to spend less money attending an expensive private school than a state institution that appears on the surface to be a bargain.

What's also overlooked by those who believe that only public schools are affordable is the cost of delays. The four-year graduation rates at many private colleges are significantly more impressive than at many public schools. When comparing the costs of a public and a private school, be realistic about how soon your child can graduate. Attending a public university for five or six years can cost the same or be more expensive than graduating from a private college in four years. That's especially true when you add in the lost financial opportunity your child will experience if he or she must delay the start of a career by one or two years.

Finding liberal arts schools. Small schools are scattered around the country. You'll find an instant list by visiting the Web site of the Annapolis Group, which is an organization of leading liberal arts colleges (www.collegenews.org/theannapolisgroup.xml). You can find more names by reading Loren Pope's book.

Action Plan

Don't overlook liberal arts colleges when exploring your options. These small schools can provide an excellent education while being just as affordable as a public university.

25

What Makes Public Liberal Arts Colleges Special

If liberal arts colleges pay attention in hiring, training, supporting and tenuring faculty, there is really no way universities, no matter how highly ranked, can match them in teaching excellence.

—Victor E. Ferrall Jr., former president of Beloit College

Believe it or not, it is possible to underwrite an undergraduate degree at a four-year public institution for a reasonable price without sharing the experience with tens of thousands of other kids. If you don't assume that bigger is always better—and many people unfortunately do—you may want to seriously investigate public liberal arts colleges.

The public liberal arts college is something of an oddity in the higher ed universe. The vast majority of liberal arts colleges in this country are private. The most prominent ones such as Amherst College, Swarthmore College, Carleton College, and Pomona College are not only pricey (if you don't qualify for financial aid), but also exclusive. State liberal arts colleges, however, are less expensive, and your child doesn't have to be an Einstein clone to gain admission.

Liberal arts colleges, whether private or state run, are focused on teaching undergraduates. The private schools typically have no graduate programs, while the state versions may offer master's degree programs. It might be somewhat misleading to say that the goal of liberal arts colleges is to encourage students to learn for learning's sake.

Obviously, these kids are interested in securing good jobs after they graduate, but you typically won't find specialized occupational programs such as nursing, pharmacy, engineering, and parks and recreation. Instead most degrees, if not all, are awarded in traditional liberal arts such as the sciences, literature, foreign languages, economics, social sciences, and history.

Because these schools offer few if any graduate degrees, the faculty is more focused on teaching undergraduates. And here's another welcome reality: There are often few, if any, graduate students teaching classes. One of the biggest draws at these schools, whether private or public, are the professors, who are not as likely to be consumed by research commitments.

One of the most noticeable features of liberal arts colleges is their size. Many private liberal arts colleges have fewer than 2,000 students. Public liberal arts colleges typically have enrollments under 5,000, which is, of course, far less than many state universities. In contrast to students at state universities, undergrads at public liberal arts colleges are more likely to attend smaller classes and develop working relationships with their professors.

Many state liberal arts outposts aren't well known. For instance, while most people have heard of Rutgers, which is the state university in New Jersey, few outside the Garden State know about The College of New Jersey, which has been called a "budget Ivy." The College of New Jersey, which possesses a higher four-year graduation rate than UCLA, attracts students with impressive academic records and standardized test scores that you routinely see at selective private schools. The middle 50% of the SAT scores for a recent incoming freshman class ranged from 570 to 670 out of a possible 800 for reading and 600 to 700 for math.

The test scores are also noticeably higher at Truman State University in Kirksville, Missouri, which is the state's only public liberal arts college, compared to the University of Missouri in Columbia, which is the state's flagship institution. Truman's focus has also been to become a public Ivy through quality teaching and challenging academics.

Some of these public liberal arts oases can be tough to get into. The College of New Jersey, for instance, turns away 56% of its applicants. Another gem, St. Mary's College of Maryland in St. Mary's City,

Maryland (a public school despite its name), rejects 44% of its applicants. Plenty of these schools, however, don't erect high barriers. Southern Oregon University in picturesque Ashland, Oregon, which is known for its Shakespeare studies and theatre, accepts 93% of its applicants. Among the many schools with high acceptance rates are Humboldt State University in Arcata, California (80%) and the University of Minnesota, Morris (80%).

Here is a list of many of the nation's public liberal arts schools:

East

The College of New Jersey, Ewing, New Jersey

Eastern Connecticut State University, Willmantic, Connecticut

Keene State College, Keene, New Hampshire

Massachusetts College of Liberal Arts, North Adams, Massachusetts

Ramapo College of New Jersey, Mahwah, New Jersey

St. Mary's College of Maryland, St. Mary's City, Maryland

State University of New York (SUNY) at Geneseo, New York

State University of New York (SUNY) at New Paltz, New York

University of Maine at Farmington, Maine

Midwest

Truman State University, Kirksville, Missouri

University of Minnesota, Morris, Minnesota

University of Wisconsin, Superior, Wisconsin

South

College of Charleston, Charleston, South Carolina

Georgia College & State University, Milledgeville, Georgia

Henderson State University, Arkadelphia, Arkansas

New College of Florida, Sarasota, Florida

University of Mary Washington, Fredericksburg, Virginia

University of Montevallo, Montevallo, Alabama

University of North Carolina, Asheville, North Carolina

University of Virginia's College at Wise, Virginia
Virginia Military Institute, Lexington, Virginia

Southwest

Midwestern State University, Wichita Falls, Texas
University of Science and Arts of Oklahoma, Chickasha, Oklahoma

West

Evergreen State College, Olympia, Washington
Fort Lewis College, Durango, Colorado
Humboldt State University, Arcata, California
Sonoma State University, Rohnert Park, California
Southern Oregon University, Ashland, Oregon
University of South Dakota, Vermillion, South Dakota

Canada

University of Alberta, Augustana campus, Camrose, Alberta

You can learn more about public liberal arts colleges by visiting the Web site of the Council of Public Liberal Arts Colleges (www.coplac.org), which promotes and supports these smaller institutions.

Action Plan

When shopping for schools, don't overlook public liberal arts colleges. If given the opportunity, many students would thrive in the more intimate learning environment.

26

Teaching Versus Research

How effectively we teach is as important as what we teach, and student learning needs to be our focus.

—James L. Melsa, dean emeritus at Iowa State University College of Engineering and president of the American Society for Engineering Education

When *U.S. News & World Report* declared that the economics department at the University of California, San Diego, had muscled its way onto the list of the nation's top 10 econ departments, it was considered quite a coup. After all, UCSD, which has only been around since 1960, had joined such august company as Harvard University, Massachusetts Institute of Technology, and Stanford University. What's' more, *U.S. News & World Report* wasn't the only publication tossing laurels to the campus that enjoys stunning views of the Pacific Ocean.

Two of its professors won the Nobel Prize in economics in 2003 for their research in econometrics. Meanwhile, *Science Watch* magazine ranked the department fifth in the country for its high impact research in the decade ending in 2005. The department is crammed with world-renowned experts who can pontificate on such subjects as microeconomic theory and the economics of oil and taxes.

The word has gotten out about this hot econ department that just happens to be located in a community of perfect weather. But what's lost in the celebration is what kind of experience an undergraduate economics major might experience at this highly regarded campus.

An increasing number of UCSD students are majoring in economics, but the staffing doesn't appear to be keeping up with the enrollment.

An article in the *San Diego Union-Tribune* in 2006 touched on the difficulties that undergraduates face. In the 1995–1996 school year, 837 undergraduates were in the economics department, but 11 years later, the number had soared to 1,900. And yet, the department wasn't much bigger than during its sleepier days. At the time the article was written, the department had 32 full-time professors, which was only five more than in 1995. Comparable economics departments typically employ 15 more faculty members and have fewer students to teach. What's more, temporary lecturers were teaching 25% of the economics classes at UCSD.

An honor student quoted in the newspaper article said she and others had complained about large class sizes and lack of access to the vaunted faculty. In fact, some upper-division economics classes, where you'd expect to have smaller numbers, were crammed with up to 150 kids.

Why do I mention UCSD's sweet and sour record? One reason is to hammer this home again: Rankings don't tell the whole story. The rankings obsession can easily obscure what is just as important as—or actually more important than—attending a school with a star-studded faculty.

While it could certainly be a wonderful opportunity to take classes in a research-intensive school that includes world-renowned scholars on the faculty, there are clearly other more prosaic matters to consider.

Will it matter if a gaggle of faculty have earned Nobel Prizes if your only contact with them would be waving from the fiftieth row of a lecture hall? Of course, it's more likely that these academic prize catches will have little to no contact with undergraduate peons. What just about any teenager wants, whether he or she selects a school with 30,000 or 1,300 students, is to have meaningful contact with teachers. And this would involve more than a professor knowing the names of the students enrolled in his class.

This desire for academic intimacy, however, collides, with some stubborn practices that proponents of quality teaching, including the Carnegie Foundation for the Advancement of Teaching, the Reinvention Center at the University of Miami, and the Washington Center for Improving the Quality of Undergraduate Education, have been railing about for a very long time.

Perhaps the most destructive and ingrained belief is that research trumps teaching. Research gets you published, gets you tenure, and gets you Nobel Prizes. Being a masterful teacher, however, might get you in trouble if you spend too much time crafting your art. If you're mentoring, you might not be conducting enough research that can attract grant money and recognition for a university.

As a general rule, it's going to be tougher for a student at a large university to experience meaningful contacts with professors. Some students, particularly those who may be shy or who are content to remain under the radar, could end up graduating without even knowing teachers well enough to ask for recommendations.

What's the solution? In Chapter 27, "Learning in a Crowd," you'll learn ways to shrink a large university down to size.

Action Plan

Don't be misled by college rankings. You won't know whether a school would be an ideal academic fit until you investigate on your own.

27

Learning in a Crowd

When you're surrounded by all these people, it can be even lonelier than when you're by yourself. You can be in a huge crowd, but if you don't feel like you can trust anybody or talk to anybody, you feel like you're really alone.

—Fiona Apple, singer

One of the greatest fears that many incoming freshmen have about attending large universities is that they will be treated like numbers. It's only natural for them to wonder whether they will get lost in the academic shuffle.

Many of them unfortunately do. According to a study by the Higher Education Research Institute at UCLA, only 28% of students at public universities graduated in four years. The number improved to 58% for the six-year graduation rate.

There are ways to make attending schools with thousands of other students more productive and meaningful. Here are some of those strategies:

Look for a university with a first-year experience. A growing number of colleges and universities are eager to help students successfully transition from high school by grouping them into so-called learning communities.

There are many different ways that schools establish learning communities. Some schools schedule groups of students, who are often freshmen, to enroll in two or more courses together. The students may take some type of freshman seminar together, as well as other classes. When the classes are linked by an interdisciplinary theme, the professors will often collaborate.

In other cases, students in a learning community will attend classes with many other students, but they will meet together in small discussion groups. At some schools, the students also live in the same dorms. The Universities of Missouri, Oregon, Washington, and Wyoming call their learning communities Freshman Interest Groups or FIGs, but they also go by other names.

Studies from the National Survey of Student Engagement, which is a nonprofit group based at Indiana University that promotes student learning, show that students in learning communities become far more engaged in school than those without the experience. These students talk more with professors and their classmates—including those they may never have met otherwise. The students not only studied more but did so in a more meaningful way.

Schools with Learning Communities

Hundreds of schools—both public and private—have organized learning communities on their campuses. Here is a partial list of public universities:

Appalachian State University, Boone, North Carolina
Arizona State University all campuses
Ball State University, Muncie, Indiana
Bowling Green State University, Bowling Green, Ohio
Evergreen State College, Olympia, Washington
Iowa State University, Ames, Iowa
Indiana University, Bloomington, Indiana
Miami University, Oxford, Ohio
Ohio State University, Columbus, Ohio
Purdue University, West Lafayette, Indiana
Saint Cloud State University, St. Cloud, Minnesota
Temple University, Philadelphia

University of Central Arkansas, Conway, Arkansas
University of Connecticut, Storrs, Connecticut
University of South Carolina, Columbia, South Carolina

You can find well more than 250 schools with learning communities by visiting the Web site of the Washington Center for Improving the Quality of Undergraduate Education, which is housed at Evergreen State College in Olympia, Washington (www.evergreen.edu/washcenter/home.asp). The center, which is a resource for educational reform, also provides a primer on what learning communities are.

Another resource to check out is The Residential Learning Communities International Clearinghouse that is compiled by Bowling Green State University. Here is its web address: http://pcc.bgsu.edu/rlcch/.

Don't be fooled by ratios. Obviously, kids have a better chance of flourishing in a class of 25 than a lecture hall of 250. Families, however, are routinely misled about the size of classes when looking at college reference books or school Web sites. The ratio of faculty to students at many universities looks great. Who couldn't live with a ratio of 13 students to one professor?

But beware of misleading numbers. In calculating the figures, universities can include professors who may only teach graduate students. And it gets worse. Some professors take a portion of their research grant money and pay back a percentage of their university salary to bail out of their teaching obligation. The school uses the money to hire a temporary person and includes both academics in the faculty count.

How can you avoid being fooled? Ignore the ratios, and ask what the average class sizes for introductory courses are, as well as for courses for upperclassmen. You should get a sense of what kind of class sizes are typical for courses offered in your intended major. Once you begin taking classes in a school within a school, such as journalism, nursing, or architecture, the academic setting can seem much smaller. Also ask whether graduate students are teaching classes and labs. Obviously, a faculty member is preferred.

Ask about undergraduate research and capstone projects. While graduate students have traditionally been the ones working with faculty on research, a growing number of schools have recognized that undergrads could greatly benefit from the same opportunity. And it's not just students in the sciences, math, and engineering who are getting the chance.

Also look for universities that offer capstone projects or courses for upperclassmen. A capstone project encourages students to apply what they have learned in their major field of study in a project where they are required to demonstrate a wide mastery of the curriculum.

Look for schools with honors colleges. An increasing number of public universities offer honors colleges. One of the more cynical reasons for the trend is to capture highly desirable students who might have private schools on their shopping lists.

An honors college tries to make an institution more personal by offering special classes, and sometimes the honor students live in the same dormitories. Before pinning your hopes on enrolling in a honors college, find out the qualifications.

Ask about the advising program. It's unrealistic to expect a student to know what academic steps are necessary to flourish, much less graduate. The task can be a lot easier and rewarding if a student can rely on a faculty advisor, preferably in his or her own major. At some universities, however, students must turn to a more impersonal advising office.

Consider a 3-2 program. Even if your child might thrive in a smaller environment, it can be extremely difficult to downsize if you expect to major in certain fields such as engineering, nursing, environmental management, and forestry.

For a child who wants to become an electrical engineer, for instance, his or her options are confined primarily to universities. Only a few liberal arts schools offer engineering degrees. Schools inside that tiny cohort include Harvey Mudd College in Claremont, California; Lafayette College in Easton, Pennsylvania; Bucknell University in Lewisburg, Pennsylvania; Hope College in Holland, Michigan; Trinity College in Hartford, Connecticut; York College of Pennsylvania, York, Pennsylvania; and Smith College in Northampton, Massachusetts.

Countless liberal arts colleges, however, have tried to reach out to students, who desire a specialized major, by offering so-called 3-2 programs. Here's how these programs work: You attend a liberal arts college and take many of the prerequisites that you'd need for a more specialized degree, such as engineering. You spend three years at the college before transferring to a university which has a cooperative program.

Washington University in St. Louis; California Institute of Technology in Pasadena, California; Columbia University in New York City; Case Western Reserve University in Cleveland; and Duke University in Durham, North Carolina, are five major institutions that welcome engineering transfer students. Duke is also a major source for 3-2 alliances for forestry and environmental management degrees.

Once at the new school, a student would spend two years studying engineering. After the fifth year, the graduate would walk away with two degrees—a bachelor of arts and a bachelor of science in engineering.

A 3-2 program allows you to experience a more personalized academic setting, as well as eventually attend a top research university. You would ultimately earn a degree from a university that you may not have gotten into as a freshman. There are, however, a couple of disadvantages. Many students, once they get settled into their liberal arts college, lose any desire to move on for their senior year. The arrangement can also be costly since it will take five years to obtain two bachelor's degrees.

Action Plan

If you expect to attend a large university, look for institutions that strive to make sure that their undergraduates, and especially freshmen, don't get lost in the shuffle.

Part V

Exploring Community Colleges

28

Considering a Community College

Community colleges are the home of second chances and fresh starts, attracting students of a wide range of academic abilities and financial means.

—from the study "Transfer Access of Elite Colleges and Universities in the United States: Threading the Needle of the American Dream"

If you expect to attend a community college, it's only natural to feel left out if your friends are heading out of town for college. That was what was on the mind of a teenage girl, who posted her frustrations on the Web site of *Inside Higher Ed*.

The student lamented that her friends were all focused on leaving home and having experiences, such as living in a dorm, that she wouldn't have. "At my graduation," she wrote, "college talk was common. When people found out that I was attending the (local) community college, the response that I got more often-than-not was 'Oh? Community college? I'm sorry.'"

The teenager came to the right spot to share her angst. She received an encouraging response from a community college dean, who is a regular blogger on the Web site devoted to higher ed news. In commiserating with the student, the dean, who writes anonymously on community college issues, noted that it makes no difference where you start a college career, but it does matter what you do with the education you receive.

The dean attended what he called a SLAC (snooty liberal arts college). The price tag was so high that he didn't pay off the last loan until he was 35 years old. Here is a snippet of his advice:

> *If you're worried about beer or boyfriends, don't be. There will be plenty of opportunity for both. (A clarinetist I briefly dated once said, in apparent seriousness, "Men are like buses. If I miss one, there'll be another in fifteen minutes." I couldn't decide if that was mere callousness or comic genius.) Dorms are a lot less interesting than they're cracked up to be. Friends will be made wherever, and the upside of the tough job market for professors is that some really great professors can be found just about anywhere.*
>
> *If you go the community college route, my advice would be to demand from it the fullest experience it can offer. Join a few clubs, plug into the grapevine, look for an honors program, join Phi Theta Kappa (community college honors organization) if/when you can, get involved.*
>
> *If you choose to treat it as less than a "real college," that's what you'll get. But if you take ownership of your experience, you'll be well ahead of your peers elsewhere who drink their way through indifferent studies. And yes, you'll have much lower loan payments when you get out, which means you'll have more options. This is not to be sneezed at.*

If you're considering attending a community college, keep reading. In the next three chapters, you'll learn how to evaluate community colleges and increase your chances of being prepared for the ultimate leap to a four-year school.

Action Plan

A community college can be an excellent way to begin your college experience.

29

Why Community Colleges Are Popular

The first concern of the research university is, unsurprisingly, research. Community colleges, by contrast are far more focused on teaching, and some are doing it better than even the most esteemed four-year institutions.

—Kevin Carey, research and policy manager at Education Sector, an education think tank

While the Ivy League and other elite schools fuel much of the angst that envelops the college admission process, these elitist campuses welcome only an infinitesimal fraction of college freshmen.

By far, the largest number of kids head off to community colleges. In fact, that's where 45% of all freshmen end up. With roughly 1,200 community colleges in existence, campuses are located within commuting distance of more than 90% of Americans.

There are many reasons why so many teenagers, as well as older students, choose two-year schools. Cost is a biggie. The average tuition, according to the American Association of Community Colleges, was recently $2,272 versus $5,836 for a four-year public institution. Even with the low cost, nearly half of community college students receive financial aid.

Community colleges can also be a bargain in ways that many people completely overlook. Despite the modest cost, these colleges offer an antidote to the cavernous lecture halls that many underclassmen at state universities must tolerate. Community colleges allow students to take the same required general education classes in a far more intimate setting than those taught at universities.

With smaller classes, community college students can get to know their professors in a way that a freshman enrolled in an introductory class at a university can rarely experience. In fact, community college professors teach their own classes unlike many of their counterparts at four-year universities, where research is a primary preoccupation. It's unlikely that you will find teaching assistants at community colleges. Students at community colleges are also in a better position to elicit their teachers' help.

Community colleges are also trying to become more attractive to the sort of high school graduates who normally would hop directly to a four-year school. Motivated kids can save a ton of money by starting at a two-year school. To attract these students, an increasing number of schools are offering honors classes. Those with honors programs include Bergen Community College in Paramus, New Jersey; Miami Dade (Florida) College; Pima County Community College in Tucson, Arizona; Sinclair Community College in Dayton, Ohio; Valencia Community College in Orlando, Florida; and Joliet (Illinois) Junior College, which is considered the oldest public community college in the nation.

About 20% of the 800 institutions in the National Collegiate Honors Council, which sets standards for honors programs, belong to community colleges. You can find community colleges in the council by visiting its Web site at www.nchchonors.org.

To serve their students better, a growing number of community colleges are trashing their original mandate and turning into four-year institutions for a limited number of disciplines. Some schools, such as Miami Dade College, St. Petersburg (Florida) College, and Northern New Mexico College in Espanola, New Mexico, dropped community from their names to reflect their new mission.

Some students see community colleges as a temporary pit stop because their grades aren't good enough for the schools they covet. Through open admission policies, community colleges routinely admit anyone with a high school diploma or GED regardless of a student's standardized test scores or high school transcript.

Still others consider a two-year school as a good place to start since they have no idea what majors they might want to explore. Community colleges can also be a good fit for those who want or need to work while getting an education. Many schools have evening and online classes.

About half of community college freshmen don't intend to earn a bachelor's degree. Some community college programs don't require a two-year commitment. An amazing 50% of new nurses and the majority of other health-care workers attend community colleges.

Hottest Community College Careers

According to the American Association of Community Colleges, these are the five most popular programs on two-year college campuses:

1. Registered nursing
2. Law enforcement
3. Licensed practical nursing
4. Radiology
5. Computer technologies

Dorm Life and Community Colleges

Some students hesitate to attend a two-year school because they want to experience living on a campus. Traditionally, few community colleges offered housing, and those that did were typically confined to rural areas that draw students from a wider area than urban schools.

But that's all changing. An increasing number of schools are building dorms as they become a popular choice. According to the American Association of Community Colleges, 240 public community colleges and 70 private ones offer dormitories.

Private two-year schools are typically referred to as junior colleges and public schools are called community colleges. There are 987 public community colleges and 177 independent schools. Another 31 are tribal community colleges.

Here are just a few of the private junior colleges, some also offer baccalaureate degrees, that maintain dorms:

Alvernia College, Reading, Pennsylvania
Andrew College, Cuthbert, Georgia
Dean College, Franklin, Massachusetts
Fisher College, Boston, Massachusetts
Harcum College, Bryn Mawr, Pennsylvania
Holy Cross College, Notre Dame, Indiana
Landmark College, Putney, Vermont
Lincoln College, Lincoln, Illinois
Mount St. Mary's College, Los Angeles, California
Spartanburg Methodist College, Spartanburg, South Carolina

Action Plan

A community college can provide a more intimate and far cheaper learning experience for freshmen and sophomores.

30

Is Your Local Community College Any Good?

Prestige simply isn't synonymous with good teaching. Some unknown community colleges offer more challenging educations than do certain well-regarded four-year universities.

—Paul Glastris, editor in chief of *Washington Monthly*

How do you know whether the community college you are thinking about attending is any good? For many students that might seem like an irrelevant question. They simply pick the closest campus.

Spending time evaluating different schools, however, can make a huge difference. Studies show that above average students can prosper just about anywhere, but students who need remedial help—and there are plenty in that category at community colleges—will face a much greater chance at success at enterprising schools that excel in educating.

Unfortunately, some community colleges are nothing more than factories. Graduation rates are low, and interaction between students and professors is rare and impersonal. At other community colleges, engaged teachers and intimate class sizes energize and challenge students who are well prepared academically. The bottom line: It would be a huge mistake to assume that all community colleges are clones.

While researchers have devoted a lot of psychic energy to measuring the quality of four-year colleges and universities, precious little time has been devoted to whether quality learning is happening at community colleges. Educators at the University of Texas in Austin, however, are helping to fill this void.

University of Texas educators at the Community College Leadership Program developed national benchmarks for academic excellence at community colleges. But the program wasn't content just to develop academic benchmarks. Every year, it aims to see how schools are measuring up by conducting its so-called Community College Survey of Student Engagement (CCSSE).

Students in randomly selected classes at each participating community college fill out surveys that ask questions highly correlated with student learning and retention. Colleges use the results to examine how they are running their campuses. But the surveys can also be a goldmine to potential students since all the results are public. In contrast, the individual school results of a similar survey conducted at four-year schools, the National Survey of Student Engagement, are not always released. CCSSE provides scores for individual schools on its Web site (www.ccsse.org).

Not all schools participate in the survey, but you can use some of the same questions when evaluating community colleges. The schools are measured through five key benchmarks: active and collaborative learning, student-faculty interaction, academic challenge, support for learners, and student effort.

Here are some of the questions posted on the survey's Web site that students are asked:

Active and collaborative learning

- Did you ask questions in class or contribute to class discussions?
- Did you make a class presentation?
- Did you work with other students on projects during class?

Student-faculty interaction

- Did you discuss grades or assignments with a teacher?
- Did you talk to a teacher or advisor about career plans?
- Did you discuss ideas from your readings or classes with instructors outside class?

Academic challenge

- How many assigned textbooks, manuals, books, or book-length packs of course readings did you read in the current school year?
- How many papers or reports of any length did you write?
- How often did you work harder than you thought you could to meet an instructor's standards or expectations?

Rankings and Community Colleges

When *U.S. News & World Report*'s annual college rankings are released, community colleges are never included on the lists. Considering the controversy that the rankings fuel, that's not a bad thing. But some education insiders believe that ranking community colleges is a worthwhile pursuit.

Washington Monthly created a stir in 2007 when it published a list of what it called the 30 best community colleges in the country. Education Sector, a well-regarded education think tank, compiled the list.

Education Sector was looking for schools that fared the best in the five areas that the survey measures. The organization also independently obtained community college graduation rates. Those rates are definitely worth looking at since a minority of community college students earn a degree or certificate within three years.

The attempt to single out exemplary two-year colleges, however, created some unhappy campers. CCSSE guardians at the University of Texas wouldn't cooperate with the Education Sector. The project's director was quoted as saying that ranking community colleges was a "really dumb idea." The opponents complained that rankings would ignore important differences in two-year colleges, such as the kind of students they attract, their size, and their financial resources.

But the community college rankings are a heck of a lot different from *U.S. News & World Report*'s controversial rankings of four-year schools. The news magazine relies heavily on a school's reputation in determining its collegiate pecking order. It also places a heavy emphasis on how selective the schools are, as well as the weight of their endowments.

Education Sector has rightly criticized *U.S. News & World Report*'s rankings for failing to measure what's truly important—the learning experience for students who actually enroll. And that's why Education Sector and the *Washington Monthly*'s collaboration is valuable. Their list is dependent on what's actually happening in the classrooms.

Best 30 Community Colleges

In the *Washington Monthly*'s list, smaller colleges rose to the top. Nineteen schools have enrollments of fewer than 2,000, and eight of the institutions had fewer than 1,000 students.

1. Atlanta Technical College, Georgia
2. Cascadia Community College, Washington State
3. Southern University at Shreveport, Louisiana
4. Southwestern Community College, North Carolina
5. Hazard Community and Technical College, Kentucky
6. North Florida Community College, Florida
7. Wisconsin Indianhead Technical College, Wisconsin
8. Southeast Kentucky Community and Technical College, Kentucky
9. Zane State College, Ohio
10. Abraham Baldwin Agricultural College, Georgia
11. Texas State Technical College-Marshall, Texas
12. Lake City Community College, Florida
13. Itasca Community College, Minnesota
14. South Piedmont Community College, North Carolina
15. Vermillion Community College, Minnesota
16. Hawaii Community College, Hawaii
17. Ellsworth Community College, Iowa
18. Chipola College, Florida

19. Martin Community College, North Carolina
20. Texas State Technical College-West Texas, Texas
21. South Texas College, Texas
22. Skagit Valley College, Washington
23. Valencia Community College, Florida
24. MiraCosta College, California
25. Florida Community College at Jacksonville, Florida
26. New Hampshire Community and Technical College, New Hampshire
27. Frank Phillips College, Texas
28. Mesabi Range Community and Technical College, Minnesota
29. Northwest Vista College, Texas
30. New Mexico State University-Grants, New Mexico

Action Plan

Don't assume that the closest community college is your best bet. Refer to the questions formulated by the Community College Survey of Student Engagement when researching schools.

31

Getting Credit for Your Work

We've found a lot of institutions, particularly private institutions, don't have a lot of financial aid for transfer students. They get what's left after schools offer aid to freshmen first.

—Emily Froimson, director of Higher Education Programs at the Jack Kent Cooke Foundation

Community colleges are inexpensive, but their educational value will shrink if you never graduate. It takes the average community college student six years to obtain a two-year associate's degree. Most students who start community college never even earn a diploma.

Experts offer many reasons for the dismal track records. Some kids aren't prepared academically for college work. Some students must juggle school and work. About 63% of students are part-timers, which dramatically reduces their chances of ever finishing their associate's degree. According to the National Center for Education Statistics, only 15% of part-time students completed a degree or certificate after six years, and 73% left without one. In contrast, 64% of full-time students at community colleges walked away with a diploma within six years.

Obviously, if you start at a community college you will want to graduate in two years so you can complete your college career elsewhere. You should be thinking ahead to what you need to do to eventually transfer even before your first day at a community college. Here is what you need to do to increase your chances:

Focus on transferring credits. Students, whose ultimate aim is a bachelor's degree will want all their hard work to get counted. And that means making sure their credit hours transfer.

Ideally, attaining an associate's degree should fulfill the requirements for the first two years of a baccalaureate degree. In many states, however, graduates can't assume that a four-year institution will honor all their hard-earned credits. Four-year institutions maintain their own requirements for which community college credits transfer.

So how do you know whether your dream school will take your credits?

One way is to select a community college that maintains well-established relations with the college or university you hope to attend. For instance, the University of California system, which has a highly competitive admissions policy for freshmen, offers a popular program for the state's community college students. The vast majority of students who transfer to the UC campuses come from the state's community colleges.

The relationship between community campuses and four-year institutions is spelled out in so-called articulation agreements. In some states, such as Florida and Pennsylvania, anybody who graduates with an associate's degree in these states will be welcomed into a four-year public school in their respective state.

You can obtain a state-by-state list of articulation agreements by visiting the Web site of FinAid (www.finaid.org). Type "articulation agreement" into FinAid's Web site to locate the list.

Don't assume, however, that all these agreements involve four-year public institutions. You can find partnerships between community colleges and private colleges and universities across the country. The University of Southern California and Mount St. Mary's College, which are both in Los Angeles, for instance, honor agreements with many community colleges in California. In Pennsylvania, community colleges maintain articulation agreements with dozens of private institutions in the Keystone State such as Bucknell University, Drexel University, Widener University, Lehigh University, Lafayette College, University of Scranton, St. Joseph's University, and Villanova University.

Making sure a four-year institution will accept your credits shouldn't be your only goal. You'll want these credits to apply to your major.

Phi Theta Kappa, which is the academic honor society for two-year colleges, offers an interactive online service at CollegeFish.org to help community college students make the leap to four-year schools. It provides transfer tools to help complete a baccalaureate degree, as well as career tools.

Consult your advisor. One way to ensure that students finish their community college stint as soon as possible is to make sure they use the resources available to them. That means taking advantage of the school's academic advising counselors.

An annual survey that measures academic quality of community colleges recently concluded that far too few take advantage of counseling services. According to the Community College Survey of Student Engagement, 41% of students taking college-level courses and 26% of students taking remedial classes rarely or never take advantage of academic advising.

Look for money. Many students spend their first two years in community college because it's an inexpensive option. They may understandably wonder how they are going to pay for the last two years of school at a pricier institution.

One way to cut the cost is to look for transfer scholarships. The Jack Kent Cooke Foundation (www.JackKentCookeFoundation.org) provides the nation's largest scholarships for community college graduates. The nonprofit awards roughly 50 scholarships annually that are worth up to $30,000 a year for the winning students. Those interested in this generous scholarship can't apply directly. Students must be nominated by a faculty representative of the foundation. You can find the names of faculty reps at individual campuses by visiting the foundation's Web site.

Phi Theta Kappa is another scholarship resource for community college students. You can tap into its eScholarship Directory by visiting its Web site at www.ptk.org.

Action Plan

When attending a community college, you need to make sure that your hard-earned credits will eventually transfer.

Part VI

College Admission Nuts & Bolts

32

Knowing When to Do What

If you want to conquer fear, don't sit home and think about it. Go out and get busy.

—Dale Carnegie

Everybody knows that getting into college today is rarely effortless. But it's possible to reduce the stress level if you use this cheat sheet. Here's a list of what teenagers, and in some cases their parents, should be doing beginning in the freshman year of high school.

Freshman Year

Enroll in strong college prep courses. These classes can prepare you for the workload that awaits in college. College admissions officers want to see that you've taken challenging courses. In fact, colleges routinely put more weight on grades and the strength of your high school's curriculum than they do on standardized test scores.

Meet with high school counselor. Find out what classes you need to take during the next four years to satisfy, at a minimum, the requirements of your state universities. Also ask about academic coursework that private schools might require.

Get extra help. If necessary, find a tutor for difficult subjects and/or attend summer school.

Volunteer and join. It's easy to become cynical when contemplating what extracurricular and volunteer activities are best. A teenager should not get involved in something simply because it might grab an admissions officer's attention.

Colleges aren't necessarily going to be impressed if a teenager simply joins a bunch of high school clubs. They often are excited about kids who show initiative and leadership abilities. This most definitely doesn't mean that a child has to get involved in student government. Far from it. Kids should try linking their extracurricular activities to their passions. My daughter, for instance, had been playing soccer since third grade, so it was a natural fit for her to become a soccer coach for a kids' recreational league. She also earned money as a soccer referee for several years. In addition, she turned her love of arts and crafts into a volunteering opportunity by creating scrapbooks for assisted living facilities.

Read, read, and read some more. Being a strong reader can not only make a teenager a better student, but it can make it easier to perform well in college. Reading may also lead to higher scores on the SAT, which now places a heavier emphasis on reading ability. Reading comprehension is not something you can cram for in the weeks leading up to the test.

Sophomore Year

Consider taking the PSAT in October. Juniors typically take this pre-SAT test, but at plenty of high schools sophomores do as well. The test can provide an idea of how your child might fare with the SAT. By getting an assessment early, there is plenty of time to address a child's weaknesses.

Take SAT Subject Tests. If a teenager is interested in schools that require SAT Subject Tests, he or she should try to take the relevant subject test right after completing the high school course. SAT Subject Tests are available in such courses as U.S. history, chemistry, mathematics, foreign languages, and molecular or ecological biology. Most schools don't require these extra tests, but those that do may want scores in one to three subjects.

Keep reading! The College Board has compiled a great reading list for high schoolers, *101 Great Books*. To obtain the list, type that title into the College Board's search engine at www.collegeboard.com.

Begin researching schools. Books, such as *Fiske Guide to Colleges* and *The Princeton Review's The Best 366 Colleges* provide an overview of many brand-name schools, but the vast majority of colleges and universities aren't covered.

An online resource that covers more territory is College Confidential (www.collegeconfidential.com), which maintains countless articles about choosing colleges, paying the tab, and many more topics. The site also hosts forums on colleges and universities across the country. Parents and students can post questions about individual schools on the forums and share their impressions of institutions after they have visited.

Another resource to generate more ideas is the College MatchMaker, located on the College Board's Web site. Also check out the federal College Navigator at http://nces.ed.gov/collegenavigator. You should also visit school Web sites, attend college fairs in your area, and talk to your guidance counselor about potential schools.

Visit schools. The summer between sophomore and junior year can be a convenient time to begin checking out schools. The visits may help motivate a teenager after he or she sees what hard work can lead to.

Create a filing system. Once you begin accumulating college marketing materials, you'll need a place to organize it. Create file folders for each school that interests you.

Junior Year

Continue researching and visiting schools and taking challenging classes. Many students and teachers believe this is the hardest year for the college bound.

Study for the SAT. An inexpensive way to prepare for the test is to buy a test prep book, which you can find at just about any bookstore. A wonderful (and free) test prep resource online is www.Number2.com. What I especially like about Number2.com is that it dispatches e-mails to parents that contain a weekly progress report breaking down how many questions the child tackled, how many he got right, and how many minutes or hours he spent on the site.

Another delightful—and unique—site is FreeRice (www.freerice.com). Every time a visitor to this site gets a vocabulary word right, the site's advertisers donate 20 grains of rice to the United Nation's World Food Program. Since FreeRice was launched in the fall of 2007—by a dad helping his kids with SAT words—the site has generated donations of 19 trillion grains of rice.

An expensive option is an SAT prep class, which can cost $1,000 or more. Check to see whether your high school provides free SAT preparation.

Register for the SAT well in advance. You're taking a risk if you expect to sign up for the SAT a few days before the test. The test slots fill up, and even if you do waltz in at the last minute, the test will cost more money. You can check SAT deadlines by visiting the College Board's Web site.

Take the SAT test. A good time for many juniors to tackle the SAT is late winter, early spring. If your child is studying Algebra II as a junior, consider delaying the test toward the end of his or her junior year since this level of math is included in the test.

Consider the ACT. Some students perform better on the ACT, while others experience greater luck on the SAT. Both test many of the same skills, however, differences exist. Unlike the SAT, for instance, the ACT includes a science section, as well as trigonometry questions. The SAT places a greater emphasis on vocabulary, and it imposes a guessing penalty.

Estimate financial aid need. Use online calculators at FinAid.org and the College Board's Web site.

Write thank you notes. After visiting a school, send a note if you spoke personally to an admissions officer, professor, or coach.

Senior Year

Use a calendar. The more schools you apply to, the crazier it's going to get. The only way to keep track of college admissions and financial aid deadlines is by writing it all down on a calendar.

Work on applications. In the summer months, before the senior year gets underway, focus on applications and essays. It's just about impossible to overestimate how time consuming these tasks can be after school starts.

Get a head start on recommendations. A lot of teachers and guidance counselors are inundated with requests for recommendations after Thanksgiving. Ask teachers for recommendations in September, October, or even earlier when they will be less harried. At some private schools, teachers write recommendations in the summer months before senior year begins. Thank teachers who help with a gift certificate to a place like Starbucks or Barnes & Noble.

Retake the SAT. With deadlines looming, time is running out to try the SAT again if you aren't happy with your scores. Many schools will mix and match SAT scores. For example, suppose you received a higher score on the critical reading section and a lower math score during the first try, but the scores were reversed when taking it again. Many schools will select the highest scores among the two tries.

Complete the CSS/Financial Aid PROFILE. Mostly private schools use this online form to determine eligibility for financial aid that doesn't emanate from the federal government. You can register to use the PROFILE by visiting the College Board Web site. Some schools want this form filed before January 1.

File the Free Application for Federal Student Aid (FAFSA). Submit the FAFSA, which will be available online at the beginning of the new year, as soon as possible after January 1. If you don't have all your tax documents ready, submit an estimated FAFSA. You can submit an estimated PROFILE too.

Evaluate admissions offers. After the admissions verdicts and financial aid packages are in, families may need to do soul searching. Parents and students should talk about the financial implications of attending different schools.

Take Advanced Placement tests. If you're doing well in Advanced Placement classes, take the appropriate AP tests that are administered in May. With high scores, you may obtain college credits.

Contact the also-rans. Write or e-mail the schools that didn't make your final cut so they can extend offers to other students.

Send in the deposit. For most schools, the deadline for mailing in the enrollment form with the deposit is May 1.

Don't slack off. Even after you receive college acceptances, you should keep your grades up in the last semester. Colleges can rescind offers.

Explore lenders. Not all lenders are alike. When comparison shopping, don't limit yourself to the lenders on a school's preferred list. Use federal loans first. Private loans should be your last option.

Register for Selective Service. Young men won't be eligible for federal financial aid if they haven't registered.

Find a summer job. Get a head start on paying those college bills.

Action Plan

- Don't wait until your junior or senior year to begin preparing for college.
- It will be easier to avoid trouble by following a timeline like the one in this chapter.

33

Grading College Counselors

Colleges are no longer centered on counseling students; we are focused more on recruiting and competing for them. The students are just a way of keeping score. Furthermore, we charge different prices to students whom we value more or less because of our internal institutional priorities. Is it really any wonder that high-school counselors and families are now overwhelmed in this process?

—Don Bishop, associate vice president for enrollment management at Creighton University

During one summer vacation, *BusinessWeek* ran an article about private college counselors who charge families as much as a new Lexus to advise them. The teenagers interviewed for the story didn't want their names divulged. Perhaps they were embarrassed that their parents were spending the equivalent of a year's tuition at Harvard to, well, to get them into Harvard. The parents, however, weren't shy about writing the checks.

Some of these platinum-priced counselors seem to be as exclusive as the Ivy League schools that these clients are lusting after. Kids who the counselors feel don't measure up are turned away. To accommodate the demand, one highly sought-after counselor takes the overflow from her practice and funnels them into expensive application boot camps.

Of course, the use of these exorbitantly compensated hired guns creates the impression that only the wealthy can win the admissions race. That notion certainly displeases Thomas H. Parker, dean of admission and financial aid at Amherst College, one of the nation's premier liberal arts colleges, who wrote about his disdain for private counselors in *The Chronicle of Higher Education*: "What is important to understand about families who make use of independent college counselors is that they are both highly competitive and used to controlling their own destinies. In their eyes, the college-admissions process is reduced to little more than a contest. Furthermore, it is a contest that is to be won (perhaps at all costs) and a process that is to be tightly controlled."

Counselors who advise the phenomenally wealthy on a fee schedule that rivals attorneys have rightly received a lot of flack. But that aside, there are many experts who can be a tremendous help to families and who don't charge outrageous prices or any at all. These experts include high school counselors and independent college counselors, as well as investment advisors and Certified Public Accounts, who focus on the financial and tax aspects of paying for college and qualifying for financial aid.

Why You Might Want a Lifeline

Independent and high school counselors can be a valuable resource for families for the very reasons that the administrator at Creighton University suggests. Not all families are going to want to navigate the Byzantine world of college admissions by themselves. This is understandable because the rules of the game can change frequently. In fact, instead of being anchored to a sturdy stone foundation, the admissions and financial aid rules often seem like they are careening down a Slip 'n Slide.

Back in the early 1990s, for instance, colleges rarely gave out merit scholarships to any students who weren't academically spectacular. Many parents and kids believe that's still the status quo. But today, it's possible for solid "B" students with decent standardized test scores to walk away with merit money. Although the kid who is simply above average has a shot at money, even that common practice can't always be counted on. A college may have given merit money last year to your neighbors' son with a 3.2 grade points average and a 1100 SAT (on the le), but that doesn't mean your child, whose stats are better, ssume she'd be a shoo-in for a scholarship to the same school ear. Multiply this one example many times over, and you'll get some idea of the mercurial nature of the college process.

Just as you would when choosing a college, you have to be careful that you consult the right people. Not everybody who is eager to make a buck in this business is competent, much less ethical. What follows is a rundown on what kind of help is available.

Independent College Counselors

When searching for an independent college counselor, don't be mesmerized by a firm's touted success rate in getting kids into the Ivy League. High-profile counselors aren't turning "B" students into kids that Princeton will drool over. These advisors help academic overachievers who could get into excellent schools without anyone's help. The aim of these admissions power brokers is arguably to take these top students and turn them into the collegiate version of Stepford Wives to boost their chances even more. Under the circumstances, the success rate is meaningless.

Frankly, you should think twice about hiring any counselor who doesn't want to work with a variety of kids whether they are "C" students or future Rhodes scholars.

Another warning sign is counselors who assume that families are going to want to aim for the most prestigious school they can finagle their kids into. Let's just say this kind of knee-jerk mind-set is destructive. The ideal counselors—and there are plenty out there—will spend time learning about their clients and then exploring what kind of institutions would be best for them academically, socially, geographically, and financially.

Counselors who peddle prestige and try to Botox every blemish off a kid's record rather than finding the best fit encourage what amounts to "child abuse." That's the opinion of Carolyn Z. Lawrence, a wonderful independent college counselor in San Diego County. If a counselor promises she can mold a kid into the perfect candidate, Lawrence says, you should run.

Producing the perfect teenager all too often requires children to surrender much of their high school lives. They are pressured to take classes or assume extracurricular activities that don't interest them or will consume far too much time and provoke too much anxiety.

Finding a College Counselor

College experts aren't clones; they offer different talents. Who you consult will depend on what you want. Some independent counselors, for instance, specialize in admission strategies. They are familiar with the requirements of many campuses, and they keep track of what these institutions are looking for and what scholarships and financial aid are available. These counselors have spent a great deal of time visiting campuses. You don't want somebody, by the way, who gets her information about individual schools strictly from the same books that you can buy.

Other experts may specialize in filling out the financial aid forms or working on financial aid appeal letters. They may offer families advice on how they can increase their chances for financial aid or use other strategies for paying the tab. Some counselors are excellent resources for students with disabilities.

To increase your chances of getting a qualified counselor, consider looking for experts, who belong to one of these professional groups:

- **Independent Educational Consultants Association**, www.educationalconsulting.org
- **Higher Education Consultants Association**, www.hecaonline.org

You can search for counselors by using each organization's online directories.

The Cost of Advice

If you eliminate the high profile counselors, many counselors do not generate obscene bills. I've talked to wonderful counselors who only charge a few hundreds dollars. And when you think what colleges cost, being pointed in the right direction can be well worth the price.

For those who'd love the advice of a counselor without writing a check, I'd urge you to visit AdmissionsAdvice.com. This Web site, created by Carolyn Z. Lawrence, is an incredible font of information on any topic related to choosing and evaluating schools. Spending time browsing the Web site's archives will provide you with a tremendous education. Lawrence also maintains discussion boards on her site where you can pose questions, as well as get the viewpoints of other parents. When I last checked, the discussion boards had covered more than 1,650 topics.

High School Counselors

With colleges dramatically changing the way they do business, high school counselors can provide an invaluable service to their students. For most students, the high school counselor is the only expert they will ever consult, so it's important to get as much face time as necessary with him or her.

High school counselors will know the admission successes and misfires of their graduates. They should also know which schools have been financially generous to their high school seniors. The most valuable counselors will direct students to schools they might not have ever considered. Counselors also routinely update scholarship opportunities, and they will maintain a schedule of colleges and universities that will be visiting their high schools. They can also advise students about whether the classes they are taking are appropriate for the type of schools they hope to attend.

You obviously will want as much help as possible from a school counselor, but you also have to realize that many are overworked. Their work day is often consumed with juggling the needs of hundreds of kids as they herd them through the college process that imposes unforgiving deadlines for applications, scholarships, and financial aid. Just filling out college recommendations for all their charges can keep counselors busy well past school hours and into the weekends.

Keeping this in mind, students should make life as easy as possible for their counselors. An excellent way to do this is to ask for the college recommendations that you need well in advance. At many high schools, counselors are deluged with recommendation requests in November or December. Get yours in earlier. If you're applying to any school through early decision or early action, submit your request even sooner.

Find out what your counselor needs to complete your recommendation. He or she might want a list of your strengths, your educational and career goals, and why you want to attend a particular college. You should also provide a concise description of each school. The more personalized the recommendation, the better.

You should provide copies of the recommendation form, as well as preaddressed and stamped envelopes. Also express your gratitude to your counselor with a note and—even better—a gift card to Starbucks, a restaurant, bookstore, or theater.

While high school counselors are valuable resources, keep in mind that not all of them have kept up with the times. Some counselors steer kids away from excellent schools with high price tags because they assume that their families can't possibly afford them. What they don't necessarily appreciate is that for bright students who pick wisely an expensive school can sometimes end up costing less than a public university.

Some counselors also encourage kids to apply to "reach" schools without appreciating the financial consequences of their advice. This often leads to kids combing *U.S. News & World Report* to find colleges where they might barely qualify for admission. If these kids are "lucky" enough to get into a reach school, they might find that the school is unwilling to award them any money at all. There are plenty of academic sugar daddies out there for all sorts of students, but you have to know where to look.

Action Plan

- Get the most out of your own high school counselor. School counselors can be a great resource.
- Private college counselors can be invaluable, but make sure your interests mesh with the counselor's objectives.

34

Ditching the SAT

Many colleges and universities around the country, in dropping their test score requirements, have recently confirmed what the research has shown all along—the SAT has little value in predicting future college performance.

—The National Center for Fair & Open Testing

Every parent knows that many teenagers don't test well. Some are slow readers. Others freeze when they are stuck in a room with a test booklet and well-sharpened No. 2 pencils. Some kids ace the reading section and stink on any math question that requires more than a working knowledge of Algebra 1. Still others are handicapped by their high schools, which don't prepare them as well as schools with very high academic standards and a boatload of Advanced Placement class offerings.

In the face of growing criticism about the test's relevance and fairness, a critical mass of schools now offer an escape route. Hundreds of colleges and universities—and the list seems to grow weekly—have made the SAT and ACT optional.

The SAT dropouts include some of the most highly regarded schools in the country, including Bowdoin College, Mount Holyoke College, Pitzer College, Middlebury College, and the University of Texas at Austin. In fact, nearly a third of the schools that belong on the *U.S. News & World Report*'s list of the top 100 liberal arts schools have instituted an SAT or ACT-optional policy.

Before shouting for joy, you need to know what this means. Some colleges aren't as generous with the test-challenged as it might seem. Schools, for example, may only waive the test for students who meet a minimum grade point average or who have reached a certain class rank, such as in the top 10% of the student's graduating class. Certain schools make teenagers without test scores submit samples of graded work from their junior and senior year.

It used to be that choosing the SAT-optional route wouldn't work for many students because some colleges and universities wouldn't award merit money for students who skipped the Saturday morning SAT ritual.

Members of the National Association for College Admissions Counseling, however, overwhelmingly endorsed the position that member schools can't use minimum scores as the sole criterion for accepting students or determining who gets scholarships and financial aid. That new standard went into effect for the 2008–2009 school year.

While some schools, such as Bates College in Lewiston, Maine, dropped the SAT requirement back in the 1980s, skeptics argue that plenty of the latecomers have ditched the SAT for cynical reasons. If a school, for instance, eliminates the SAT requirement, it could experience a sizable bump in the number of applications it receives. When word gets out about the change in policy, kids with lackluster (or even very good but not phenomenal) test scores will conclude that they now may qualify for a school that they once considered an impossibility.

Schools are delighted when they receive more applications because it can help the institution claw its way up on *U.S. News & World Report's* college rankings list. How does that happen? When a school is deluged with applications, it can reject far more kids. As perverse as this may seem to many anxious families, the magazine gives brownie points to schools that reject the greatest percentage of applicants. As I said, this is the cynic's take on the SAT-optional phenomenon.

Here's another reason why industry insiders suggest that the motivation of some schools is suspicious. If a school makes the SAT optional, the institution's average SAT score for its incoming freshmen class should improve. After all, many of the kids with lackluster scores won't send them along. And guess what? *U.S. News & World Report* and other college guide books reward schools that can brag about higher SAT scores since they don't care how these figures are generated.

In an op-ed piece in *The New York Times*, Colin S. Diver, the president of Reed College in Portland, Oregon, provided this withering take on the SAT-optional trend: "I sometimes think I should write a handbook for college admission officials titled, 'How to Play the *U.S. News & World Report* Ranking Game, and Win!' I would devote the first chapter to a tactic called 'SAT optional.'" Diver called the move toward SAT optional admissions a "disheartening" trend. He said: "In the rush to climb the pecking order, educational institutions are adopting practices, and rationalization for those practices, unworthy of the intellectual rigor they seek to instill in their students."

Regardless of a school's ulterior motives, supporters of dropping the SAT requirement insist that it will make the college admission process fairer. It would open up more schools to minority applicants, as well as those from less affluent households. (Of course, a school could be more inclusive simply by giving less weight to the tests for certain applicants or for everybody who applies.) It would also help level the playing field among those who can afford expensive SAT tutoring and classes and those whose only preparation is a good night's sleep.

One of the leading SAT critics is the National Center for Fair & Open Testing (FairTest), which is a nonprofit dedicated to fighting standardized testing. It argues that SAT scores are a lousy predictor of how a student will fare at college and whether a student will graduate. Despite significant differences in instructional quality at high schools, FairTest maintains that better predictors of success are high school grade point averages and class rank.

After living with the SAT optional policy for more than two decades, Bates College in Maine has accumulated extensive data that shows that its students' performance remains strong. After gathering five years of data on its experience, Hamilton College concluded that the students who don't submit their test scores do slightly better academically than their peers.

In all likelihood, the SAT/ACT debate will never end. And in some respect the arguments—pro and con—aren't relevant to an individual student, who is trying to figure out where to apply. But what is worth thinking about is whether a high schooler should walk through the SAT-optional door. Based strictly on your grades, you may be able to win a fat admittance package from a school like Sarah Lawrence College or Bates College, but you need to think about whether an academically elite school is the right fit. If you got a 510 on the English portion of the SAT—that was recently the national average score—can you write cogent papers at an elite school?

You can obtain a comprehensive list of SAT and ACT-optional schools by visiting the Web site of FairTest, (www.fairtest.org). The schools on the list, according to the organization, "de-emphasize" the use of standardized testing. To survive the cut, schools must make admission decisions about a substantial number of applicants without relying on the ACT or SAT. Recently, more than 750 schools were on the growing list.

Here is a small sampling of the wide variety of schools that made the list:

Arizona State University, Tempe, Arizona
Austin Peay State University, Clarksville, Tennessee
Bard College, Annandale-on-Hudson, New York
Bennington College, Bennington, Vermont
Bluefield State College, Bluefield, West Virginia
Bowdoin College, Brunswick, Maine
Cazenovia College, Cazenovia, New York
Connecticut College, New London, Connecticut
Denison University, Granville, Ohio
Dickinson College, Carlisle, Pennsylvania
Drew University, Madison, New Jersey
Eckerd College, St. Petersburg, Florida
Emporia State University, Emporia, Kansas
George Mason University, Fairfax, Virginia
Gettysburg College, Gettysburg, Pennsylvania
Grambling State University, Grambling, Louisiana
Goucher College in Baltimore, Maryland
Green Mountain College, Poultney, Vermont

Hamilton College, Clinton, New York
Indiana State University, Terre Haute, Indiana
Julliard School, New York, New York
Knox College, Galesburg, Illinois
Lake Forest College, Lake Forest, Illinois
Lewis and Clark College, Portland, Oregon
McDaniel College, Westminster, Maryland
Pitzer College, Claremont, California
Portland State University, Portland, Oregon
Prescott College, Prescott, Arizona
Providence College, Providence, Rhode Island
Rollins College, Winter Park, Florida
St. John's College Santa Fe, New Mexico and Annapolis, Maryland
Texas A&M University, several campuses
University of Arkansas, several campuses
University of Idaho, Moscow, Idaho
University of Iowa, Iowa City, Iowa
University of Kansas, Lawrence, Kansas
University of Maine, several campuses
University of Memphis, Memphis, Tennessee
University of Montana, Missoula, Montana
University of Oklahoma, Norman, Oklahoma
University of Wisconsin, several campuses
Wheaton College, Norton, Massachusetts
Worcester Polytechnic Institute, Worcester, Massachusetts
York College, York, Nebraska

While many schools still require SAT scores, some have reduced the value of these scores. To get an idea of how crucial the SAT or ACT score is, ask an admissions officer whether the standardized scores are less important than in the past. Contact individual schools to learn what their specific standardized test policies are.

Obviously, it's better if a student has high standardized test scores and excellent grades in high school. But for kids who can't pull off that feat, schools typically put more stock on grades than standardized test numbers.

Action Plan

If you perform poorly on the SAT, consider applying to schools where the test isn't required.

35

Writing Your Way into College

The role of a writer is not to say what we all can say, but what we are unable to say.

—Anaïs Nin, author

On a sunny autumn day in San Diego, scores of college guidance counselors from across the country resisted the temptation to walk along the city's famous beaches. Instead they grabbed seats in a chilly, windowless room. The counselors, who were attending the College Board's annual convention, had shown up for one reason—to learn the secrets of writing a successful college essay.

Not surprisingly, the room was jammed. With top schools so competitive, many ambitious kids assume that if they write a zinger of an essay, it just might keep their application from getting fed into a paper shredder. So everyone—from kids, to parents, to counselors—is eager to know just what a winning essay looks like.

The speakers at the College Board session included administrators at Kenyon College in Gambier, Ohio, and Yale University in New Haven, Connecticut, which keeps 20 staffers busy reading 50 essays a day, six days a week during application season.

Here is what they had to say:

Avoid the thesaurus. Don't write like a pedantic humanities professor who is trying too hard to impress colleagues. Avoid ostentatious words that you would normally never touch. One presenter at the College Board session provided this real, over-the-top example of an overstuffed essay:

> Hi my name is Jim, and since brevity is the soul of wit I will meekly attempt to convey to you a succinct summary of my ephemeral existence. Allow me amnesty as I am often a bit alliterative. Time is of the essence throughout humankind, and with every word I write, the nearly endless ebb of extravagant expressions flow like a rushing river, fleeing futilely towards an irrelevant ocean. Dam!
>
> Don't write like that!

Skip the English paper. Too many high school English teachers encourage their kids to write with as much creativity as a cardboard box. They don't do their kids any favors by insisting that they follow stilted formulas. For instance, when students write the classic persuasive essay, they are supposed to stuff the pros and cons on a subject, whether it's abortion or the Iraq war, in the very first paragraph. High schoolers are often penalized if they deviate from that formula even if they pen a far more compelling essay.

High school teachers often chastise kids who dare to use "first person" in their papers. Colleges, however, are eager to experience an applicant's "voice" in an essay, which means writing in first person is essential. The Yale speaker at the College Board gathering called essays written in third person "scary."

Be specific. Students tend to be too vague when writing essays. A teenager might write, for instance, that his teacher is "nice." Nice is a nearly meaningless adjective. When journalists interview neighbors about an apprehended serial killer, inevitably they say that he was a "nice guy." Substitute vague generalities for details, details, details.

Deliver a take-home message. You can write a serious essay, a humorous one, a clever one. There is no right way, but you have to make sure that your essay reflects back on you. The Yale speaker observed that a lot of Ivy League wannabes write about Winston Churchill without ever tying the essay back to themselves. If you write about Darfur, what does that have to do with you? And simply writing that you feel outraged or helpless won't cut it.

Whether you are talking about cleaning a beach, babysitting, or revealing that you're gay, the essay must provide a strong sense of self. Your personality must emerge. And it should reflect what kind of person you are now. Not the person you might have been when your house was damaged by a hurricane when you were 10-years-old or when you got lost at Disneyland at the age of six.

At the College Board session, the experts shared examples of amusing essays that were very entertaining—and would have worked—if each of them had conveyed what kind of person the writer was. One essay involved a guy whose last name was Weiner. As in hot dog. The essay was clever, but it was missing that one key element.

The presenters voiced the same complaint about a creative essay that started out with this grabber sentence:

> I have ridden a pig.
>
> Stay with me here. I mean this in the most literal sense possible. I. Rode. A pig.
>
> I was four. We were visiting my Mom's family friends on their farm. They had a hog that was roughly the size of a fridge, if you knocked that fridge over and gave it a horrible stink. Mom's friend thought it would be just grand if I rode it awhile. I was smallish, and the hog was huge-ish...surely this was a no-brainer.

Stay away from the pack. I once heard an administrator at the University of San Diego speak about the thousands of college essays that he'd read over the years. What irritated him was the tendency of high schoolers to embrace the same hackneyed subjects.

Every year, applicants deluge him with essays about volunteering to build houses for poor families in Tijuana. Obviously, this is a regional phenomenon. While many kids in Southern California help with projects in Mexico, it's unlikely that you'll see kids from Minnesota there. But every region of the country is going to have kids writing essays about subjects that have been covered ad nauseam.

Here's the administrator's other pet peeve: Kids writing about their sports teams. And he is hardly alone. Frankly, nobody is going to care—except a college's athletic coaches—if you're on a nationally ranked team or you kicked the winning soccer goal of the biggest game of the century or you swatted more home runs than anybody in your high school's history.

Once again, what matters is composing an essay that speaks to who you are.

Don't be careless. Roughly 300 schools, almost all private, now let students apply for college by filling out just one standardized form that's called the Common Application (www.commonapp.org). Obviously, completing one application for multiple schools cuts down on the hassle factor. Even better, a student can use one essay to satisfy the writing requirement for all these schools.

The one-stop application process, however, can cause students to make embarrassing mistakes. Admissions officers everywhere can tell you about kids who express their deep desire to attend a competing school in their essay. These applicants forgot to swap out the name of one school for another before sending the application electronically.

Common application essay questions. These are the recent essay topics posed by schools that rely on the Common Application:

- Evaluate a significant experience, achievement, risk you have taken, or ethical dilemma you have faced and its impact on you.
- Discuss some issue of personal, local, national, or international concern and its importance to you.
- Indicate a person who has had a significant influence on you, and describe that influence.
- Describe a character in fiction, a historical figure, or a creative work (as in art, music, science, and so on) that has had an influence on you, and explain that influence.
- A range of academic interests, personal perspectives, and life experiences adds much to the educational mix. Given your personal background, describe an experience that illustrates what you would bring to the diversity in a college community, or an encounter that demonstrated the importance of diversity to you.
- Topic of your choice.

Give yourself time. The summer leading up to your senior year in high school is an excellent time to tackle application essays. Once school starts, college deadlines will whiz by.

When an essay is finished, however, you shouldn't necessarily relax if you are relying on the Common Application. While it's true that you can pen one essay for all the schools that share the Common cation, schools also often require answers to supplemental essay tions. These additional questions might not require as much effort as the main essay, but they can be time consuming. If you visit the Common Application Web site, you'll be able to determine which schools require supplemental writing. Start working on your answers well in advance of the deadlines.

If schools on your list don't use the Common Application—and most public institutions don't—become familiar with their essay requirements, if any, well in advance.

Proofread the essay. It's okay to ask a parent, friend, or teacher to review your essay. In fact, it's important to let someone else check it to make sure it doesn't contain typos and grammatical errors. You should resist, however, letting anyone change your essay so that your own voice is lost.

Get inspired. No one—except perhaps a few English majors—is going to be eager to start THE essay. Think of ways to make the process easier. If you like Starbucks, buy a Venti Mocha before you get started. If you love chewing Juicy Fruit gum, buy a fresh pack. And while you're at it, find a literary spark plug. Is there a writer or author who you especially enjoy reading? If so read a page or two before you begin or when you get stuck.

To get inspired, you may also want to look at compelling essays. *The New York Times Magazine*, in a weekly feature called Lives, prints a wonderful first-person essay every Sunday that you can find on its last page. Another resource is the *This I Believe* essays posted on National Public Radio's Web site at www.npr.org. To find them, type "This I believe" into the site's search engine.

Action Plan

Don't assume that your essay should be written like an English paper. Avoid using a stilted approach and write from your heart.

36

Visiting Campuses

Welcome, prospective students. I'm here to show you a very superficial version of what your life could be like for the next four years because I need the money.

—Anonymous tour guide, CollegeHumor.com

One of the best ways to know whether a college or university is going to be a comfortable fit is to visit it. Of course, there are plenty of other reasons to spend time on a campus. Visits are also a good way to help judge whether a school is worth its price tag. What's more, some schools bestow an admissions advantage on students who take the time to tour their campuses and talk with admissions officers. Before touring any college campuses, here are some things to keep in mind:

Think about timing. Sure, visiting colleges during the summer is convenient for students, but don't expect to encounter the real college experience. Many liberal arts colleges, for example, will be just about deserted. And don't assume that universities will exude the same feel that you'd get on an autumn day or the first warm day in spring when the quadrangle is packed with sunbathers. Even the dorms won't look the same. They could be empty or staged with Bed, Bath & Beyond decor.

If you plan a visit when a school's in session, you may be able to arrange for your child to spend the night in a dorm and sit in on classes. Colleges and universities generally recommend that you contact them two weeks in advance to book tour reservations. The easiest way to learn about a college's visitation opportunities is to check its Web site.

Take notes. If you visit more than a couple of campuses during a trip, the details will blur quickly. Which school, you may wonder, said 90% of its students receive some sort of financial aid or academic grants? Which one boasted that 60% of its students study abroad? If your child doesn't take notes, she might end up only remembering things that don't mean squat. My daughter, for example, remembered that the turkey sandwich she inhaled at the cafeteria at Willamette University in Salem, Oregon, tasted better than the one she ate at Whitman College in Walla Walla, Washington.

Urge your child to write down his or her observations after each visit. A good time to do that will be in the car while driving to the next college.

Don't over do it. Logistically, it's going to be impossible to visit more than two campuses in one day. And you'll only be able to squeeze in one campus a day if your child intends to take a tour, show up for an information session, meet with an admissions officer, and attend a class.

Know your place. Parents, who are often the ones bankrolling a child's education, might be eager to ask questions during campus tours. But it's best to encourage your child to be the one posing most of them.

Get organized. Visiting colleges can trigger more mail. When my daughter returned from college tours to the East Coast and the Pacific Northwest, she received handwritten notes from the admissions officers she had talked with. The mailbox was also stuffed with more literature that was prompted by the visits.

My daughter bought a large filing box from the office supply store so she could keep a folder for each college. When the trip is finished, your child should also send thank you notes to any admissions and financial aid officers that she met.

Of course, even before you embark on college trips, it's good to start a filing system for the deluge of college mail your son or daughter will be receiving.

Lighting a fire. Ultimately, a college trip should help your child become acquainted with what lies ahead. It may motivate him or her to focus on the ultimate prize—finding a great academic fit at a reasonable price.

Try virtual tours. Don't feel badly if you can't afford to visit as many schools as you'd like. A student can compensate by making sure a school knows he's interested. Schools often track every contact a child or parent makes with the school, whether it's a request for literature, a call to the financial aid office, or a conversation during a college fair. Meanwhile, you can get an idea of what schools look like by taking virtual tours, which many colleges offer on their Web sites.

Action Plan

To get the most out of your visits, plan well enough ahead and don't rush through the time spent on campuses.

37

Acing the College Interview

I love talking about nothing. It is the only thing I know anything about.

—Oscar Wilde, novelist and dramatist

During an interview at Dickinson College in Carlisle, Pennsylvania, the head of admissions asked my daughter Caitlin this question: "What is the most creative thought you've ever had?"

Caitlin's first panicked thought was this: "What? I have no idea." Then her brain kicked in, and she blurted out something about chopsticks. She told the dean that she wanted to learn how to use chop sticks with her left hand because she thought this would impress colleges.

Was this a silly answer? Absolutely. But Caitlin figured that answering the question was far better than hemming and hawing and ultimately punting on it. And looking back, she believes that this was the turning point in the interview. The dean seemed to be intrigued by my gregarious daughter's enthusiasm for eating Kung Pao chicken left-handed, and he continued to ask her questions 35 minutes longer than the interview was scheduled to last.

The point of sharing this anecdote is to drive home this point: There aren't necessarily right and wrong answers in a college interview. Admissions officers don't want kids to fail. They like teenagers or they would have chosen another occupation.

Admissions staffers strive to extract from kids a sense of who they are. They want a student's personality to shine through. Did my daughter even intend to practice eating left handed? No. But the answers she provided during the interview showed that she is self-confident, a quick thinker, and an entertaining storyteller. It wasn't so much what she said, but how she said it. Months later, she received an acceptance letter from Dickinson, along with a merit scholarship.

As you anticipate spending face time with admissions officers, here are some things to keep in mind to increase the chances of having productive and successful interviews:

Ask about interview opportunities. Many large public universities don't have the luxury of conducting one-on-one interviews with potential students. Because of the large numbers of applicants, their admission policies are often largely dictated by a child's grade point average and standardized test scores. But that's not the case with plenty of private colleges and universities, which take a more holistic approach.

Before visiting a school, ask whether interviews are available or required. If the answer is yes, find out which kind are conducted. Some schools use informational interviews that allow students to ask the interviewer questions about their institutions. Typically, the admissions officer does not fill out a written evaluation of the meeting and so your admission file will not mention what took place.

In contrast, many schools rely on an evaluative interview. These interviews can be stressful because the admissions officer will typically write an interview summary afterward. At these schools, the interview is just one of many factors considered beyond grades and test scores. The caliber of a student's school, extracurricular activities, admission essay, recommendations, and the applicant's level of interest, her character, and whether her relatives are alumni may all be considered.

Some schools require interviews, but they don't always need to take place on the campus. Some schools use regional admissions officers or alumni to conduct interviews at hotels in other parts of the country.

Prepare for the interview. The best way to sabotage an interview is to show up knowing little if anything about the school. If your knowledge of a school is nil, an admissions officer is going to wonder why you're sitting in his office. What's more, interviews aren't one sided. While you will be expected to answer questions, this is also a time for you to elicit information about the campus from your host. If you don't know enough to ask intelligent questions, you're in trouble.

Dress appropriately. There's definitely no need to wear a suit and tie to interviews, but you should look like a well-dressed college student wearing comfortable clothes. (Be sure they are ironed.)

Watch the slang. Don't pepper your conversation with "um," "you know," and "like." Practice ahead of time to try to eliminate these sorts of words from your conversation. And during interviews, don't slouch, stare at the floor, play with your hair, or display other nervous mannerisms.

Ask intelligent questions. During campus visits, use the opportunity to pose meaningful questions. While you might want to know whether the school has a vegan meal plan or which is the best dorm, often the most valuable questions go unasked. A great source for more insightful questions comes from the National Survey of Student Engagement (NSSE), which is trying to be a welcome alternative to the ratings frenzy perpetrated by *U.S. News & World Report*'s annual college guide.

Unlike *U.S. News & World Report*'s publication, the NSSE is curious about what kids learn after they are enrolled in schools. You should download a handy brochure, *A Pocket Guide to Choosing a College: Are You Asking the Right Questions?*, from the NSSE's Web site at http://nsse.iub.edu/html/students_parents.cfm. The questions in the brochure focus on such areas as student and faculty interaction, academic workload, and class collaboration.

Be yourself. Don't pretend to love Leo Tolstoy and William Shakespeare if you're into science fiction novels and Japanese comic books. Resist trying to figure out what you suspect are the "right" answers; you don't want to sound phony. The interview is a time to brag about what you've accomplished without sounding conceited. On the flip side, you should put the best light on any black marks tarnishing your record such as a "D" in honors calculus class. And before the interview starts, take a deep breathe!

Action Plan

Research a school before an interview and be prepared to ask intelligent questions. During the interview be sure to relax.

38

Getting In at the Last Minute

Never leave that till tomorrow what you can do today.

—Abraham Lincoln

Whoops. What if your child messes up? What if every school he or she applies to turns him down? Or what if your child is a procrastinator who overlooked a bunch of admission deadlines?

Don't worry. You probably haven't missed them all. Plenty of schools continue taking applications after the traditional May 1st admission response deadline. In fact, some public universities and community colleges will accept applications well into the summer. What's more, many schools, which impose spring deadlines, will ignore them if they haven't met their freshman quota.

How do you find schools that still have room? Check the Web site of the National Association for College Admission Counseling (www.nacacnet.org). Each year hundreds of colleges and universities notify the trade organization if they are still looking for freshmen.

The organization's Space Availability Survey: Openings for Qualified Students breaks schools down by state. For the 2007–2008 school year, for example, 292 schools notified the association of vacancies for freshmen and/or transfer students. When I looked at Pennsylvania schools on the list, I found 30 colleges and universities, including Drexel University, Susquehanna University, the University of Pittsburgh, and a couple of Penn State campuses. Florida still had openings at 11 schools including Eckerd College, Flagler College, and Barry University. In Texas, the University of Dallas and Baylor

University were among the eight schools still looking. The survey also shares whether a school can still offer institutional financial aid and whether dormitory rooms are available.

Some schools will be wary of latecomers. Consequently, your child should be prepared to provide a good explanation of why he or she is in a lurch. Your teenager also has to be the one who places the call to a school. Don't assume getting into one of these schools will be a shoo-in. Often the earlier birds experience an easier time winning admittance than the ones who procrastinate until summer. But it may be worth a try.

Action Plan

There is hope for students who overlooked all the deadlines or received rejection letters from everybody. In the spring and summer, check the Web site of the National Association for College Admission Counseling (www.nacacnet.org) for schools with vacancies.

Part VII

College Diversity

39

Diversity Blueprint

At a time when more and more low-income and minority students are preparing for college, it is disturbing that many of our most prestigious colleges and universities are turning away from them.

—Kati Haycock, director of the Education Trust

Just in time for the 2007 holiday season, *The Journal of Blacks in Higher Education* released a damning study that revealed the inner scrooge of many of the nation's most respected colleges and universities. While schools like Yale and Princeton have received kudos for their willingness to pick up the tab for low-income students, the amount they spend on this effort is a pittance. In recent years, *The Journal of Blacks in Higher Education* concluded that the percentage of minorities and other lower-income students attending almost all of the highly selective schools has shrunk.

One reason for the illusionary benevolence is because Ivy League schools and many of its peers are hardly being inundated by underprivileged overachievers who qualify for an all-expense-paid trip to an elite college. A smart kid attending a failing inner city high school is going to have a hard time producing anything approaching the polished academic resumes of kids who attend the nation's finest private and public high schools, much less those who can afford SAT tutors, internships, summers abroad, and private college counselors.

What's more, it doesn't occur to many less fortunate students who have great potential to even apply to a school like Harvard. In fact, Ivy League institutions have taken tremendous flak from other school administrators, who complain that these elite institutions are making pathetic efforts to find and reward these talented students.

In a scathing essay, Daniel F. Sullivan, the president of St. Lawrence University in Canton, New York, made this observation: "The wealthiest colleges and universities—those that can best afford the financial aid necessary to enroll a large number of low-income students—in fact enroll the smallest percentage of such students."

It's not just the Ivies, however, that are paying lip service to welcoming promising minorities into the fold. The Education Trust, a nonpartisan think tank, has concluded that college and governmental practices have made graduation rates for minorities and poor students worse than they were 30 years ago. In another study, the think tank documented that the nation's 50 flagship universities are disproportionately serving fewer of these students than in the past.

The landscape for college-bound minorities is hardly all bleak. Plenty of financial and academic opportunities exist for them, but they need to know where to look.

Graduation Rates

When evaluating schools, any high school student should examine graduation rates at individual institutions. Nobody relishes paying tuition for more than four years, but some schools do a better job of timely graduation than others. What's even worse is when students abandon college with no diploma, but plenty of student loans.

Studies have shown that the graduation issue is even more crucial for minority students. At public flagship universities across the country, for instance, 68% of white students graduate in six years, but only 58% of minorities cross the finish line.

Money explains one possible reason for the disparity. Flagship universities are using more of their money to persuade affluent students with impressive academic profiles—residents and nonresidents—to attend their schools. That's left less money to underwrite the education of students whose families truly can't afford to pay the tab. Between 1995 and 2003, flagship and other research-intensive public universities decreased grant aid by 13% to families with incomes of $20,000 or less while they boosted assistance to families making more than $100,000 by 406%.

To pinpoint which flagship schools have done a better job of serving minorities and lower-income students, consider reading the Education Trust's report, *Engines of Inequality: Diminishing Equity in the Nation's Premier Public Universities*. (Just Google the title.) The think tank rates each state's flagship school on such things as its access to minority students and the students' success while enrolled.

Another excellent resource is the Education Trust's College Results Online software at www.collegeresults.org. I mention this wonderful tool elsewhere in the book, but one feature can be particularly valuable to minority students.

The software allows you to see what the overall graduation rate is for a school, as well as a graduation breakdown for students who are Asian, African American, Latino, Native American, and white. What's more, it compares those graduation rates with similar institutions.

As an example, I randomly picked the University of Georgia, which happens to have managed an admirable parity between the graduation rate for the entire student body and its minority students. For instance, 42.5% of Georgia students graduated in four years compared with 43.5% of the school's minorities. In six years, 73.2% of students graduated while 68.9% of minority students did.

The software also showed how Georgia stacked up with 25 of its closest peers. Georgia's track record looked great compared to many other public universities. At the University of Wisconsin, for instance, 41% of students obtained a diploma in four years, but only 22.5% of minorities did. At the University of Iowa, 37.9% of students graduated in four years versus just 20.1% for minorities. The biggest gap belonged to the University of Illinois at Urbana-Champagne, where 60.3% of students completed their studies in four years compared with 36.5% of minorities.

Using another measure, however, the Education Trust's report on inequality awarded the University of Georgia an "F" for minority access to its school. Minorities recently made up 7% of the school's freshman class, but they represented 36% of the state's high school graduates.

Look Beyond the Names

Why do minority students fare better at certain schools and flounder at others? Some institutions believe it's just a matter of selectivity; less qualified students jeopardize their graduation track records. Consequently, some schools assume that raising admission requirements will help resolve the problem.

The Pell Institute for the Study of Opportunity in Higher Education strongly rejects that mind-set. In the report *Demography Is Not Destiny: Increasing the Graduation Rates of Low-Income College Students at Large Public Universities*, the institute concluded that the solution is not to become more selective. In its examination of large public universities, it discovered that some of the schools with more exclusive admission criteria and less diverse population performed worse than less selective schools. The researchers concluded that what matters is the commitment to ensuring that all students succeed. That may sound obvious to you, but it isn't necessarily so in academia.

The institute singled out these four key ways that institutions help students flourish:

Personalizing the undergraduate experience. Successful universities don't let freshmen fade into the crowd. They enroll freshmen in special first-year programs; they monitor their progress through strong advising programs and other early warning systems. They limit class size or provide supplemental instruction as an antidote to large, impersonal lecture halls.

Emphasizing the teaching mission. Unlike at many institutions, where research is most highly prized, excellent teaching is rewarded.

Creating a shared sense of community. Schools promote student involvement even on commuter campuses.

Developing an institutional culture that promotes success. That comes with strong leadership, clear goals, and a commitment of resources.

Frankly, any schools that implement these changes will benefit students of any color.

Looking Beyond the Obvious

Countless schools are eager to welcome talented, promising students of color, but many minority students limit their choices to only the most obvious picks. For instance, according to Excelencia in Education, a nonprofit policy group, about half of Hispanic undergraduate students attend just 6% of the nation's colleges and universities.

These schools are considered Hispanic-Serving Institutions (HSI) because 25% or more of the undergraduate student body are Hispanics. Places with a significant number of these institutions include campuses connected to the University of Puerto Rico, California State University, City University of New York, Los Angeles Community College District, and the University of Texas. The heavily Hispanic institutions tend to be relatively inexpensive, maintain lower admission standards, and serve students who live nearby.

Black students also frequently overlook schools that they assume cost too much or are too exclusive. *The Journal of Blacks in Higher Education*, however, has collected data over the years that documents that many prestigious liberal arts school warmly embrace black applicants. The journal compiled the following acceptance list that suggests that cracking an elite school isn't nearly as hard for a smart African American. Middlebury (Vermont) College, for instance, accepts close to three of every four black applicants, but it rejects 79% of its overall applicant pool. Williams College in Williamstown, Maryland, accepts more than half of black candidates, but turns away all but 19% of students who apply.

10-Year Black Acceptance Rate at Highly Ranked Liberal Arts Colleges

Middlebury College, Middlebury, Vermont	68%
Macalester College, St. Paul, Minnesota	65%
Carleton College, Northfield, Minnesota	58%
Oberlin College, Oberlin, Ohio	57%
Bowdoin College, Brunswick, Maine	56%
Williams College, Williamstown, Massachusetts	55%
Amherst College, Amherst, Massachusetts	53%
Colby College, Waterville, Maine	53%
Hamilton College, Clinton, New York	52%
Trinity College, Hartford, Connecticut	52%
Mount Holyoke College, South Hadley, Massachusetts	50%
Pomona College, Claremont, California	49%
Bryn Mawr College, Bryn Mawr, Pennsylvania	47%
Bates College, Lewiston, Maine	47%
Haverford College, Haverford, Pennsylvania	47%
Wellesley College, Wellesley, Massachusetts	47%
Swarthmore College, Swarthmore, Pennsylvania	46%
Vassar College, Poughkeepsie, New York	45%
Grinnell College, Grinnell, Iowa	43%
Wesleyan University, Middletown, Connecticut	41%
Claremont McKenna College, Claremont, California	40%
Smith College, Northampton, Massachusetts	39%
Colgate College, Hamilton, New York	39%
Davidson College, Davidson, North Carolina	36%

Many bright Asian students also limit their college choices, but in a different way. Many high-achieving Asians tend to apply to the same prestigious universities, such as the Ivy League schools and the premier public research institutions such as UCLA and the University of California, Berkeley. With competition fierce, Asians have accused elite schools of rejecting them for less qualified applicants simply because of their ethnicity.

College insiders debated the "Asian bias" at an annual convention of the National Association for College Admission Counseling. Panelists acknowledged that there could be some bias from teachers, counselors, and admissions officers. But they also suggested that Asians make the college admission process more difficult by tending to ignore all but the most selective research universities.

While the tendency to gravitate to the familiar is understandable, looking beyond someone's comfort zone can open many excellent possibilities. Regardless of your ethnicity, it's usually wise to cast a wide net.

Action Plan

While colleges and universities aren't as open as they should be toward minority candidates, there are plenty of opportunities for enterprising students who know where to look for a great education.

Part VIII

Economizing for College

40

Shrinking the College Tab

It is thrifty to prepare today for the wants of tomorrow.

—Aesop's Fables

The most effective way to shrink college expenses is to think big. Aim for merit awards or fat financial aid packages. There are plenty of other opportunities, however, that you can seize to whittle down costs. You'll find a lot of ideas in this chapter, as well as the next. Here are some to get you started:

Graduate in four years! It's shocking how few college kids graduate in eight semesters. Millions of students are now taking five or six years or more to earn their diplomas.

In the hall of shame, many California state universities possess dreadful four-year graduate rates, including San Jose State University (7.1%), California State University-Long Beach (10.9%), and San Diego State University (13.9%). Dismal rates are hardly confined to the West Coast. A tiny sampling of schools with terrible four-year rates include Kennesaw State University (8.3%), University of Hawaii at Manoa (11.5%), University of Louisville (12.6%), Georgia State University (13.7%), University of Utah (15.4%), University of Oklahoma (19.3%), and Western Michigan University (20.1%).

You can't just blame the terrible graduation rate on academic dead enders. At some schools, particularly public universities, classes are overloaded, and some popular degree programs require kids to spend far longer in school than they ever imagined. If a child switches a major or decides to earn a double major, the time clock can also get pushed back. The cost of college will also delay graduation because many students must work full or part time to pay the tab.

When shopping for schools, inquire about a school's four-year graduation track record. Unfortunately, the graduation rate is frequently reported as a six-year figure. As mentioned earlier, the Education Trust provides a quick way to find four-year graduation rates through its College Results Online (www.collegeresults.org). Also ask schools for the average graduation rate for particular majors. Find out why kids experience difficulty graduating on time and how the successful ones pull it off.

The following table provides a breakdown of graduation rates from a study conducted by UCLA's Higher Education Research Institute. As you'll see, different types of institutions in the study enjoyed greater success at getting their graduates out the door in a timely fashion.

Institution Type	4-Year Grad Rate	6-Year Grad Rate
Public university	28%	58%
Private university	67%	80%
Public college	24%	47%
Nonsectarian college	56%	66%
Catholic college	46%	60%
Other Christian college	51%	61%
All institutions	36%	58%

After you've chosen a school, make sure you meet as soon as possible with an academic advisor. Learn what the requirements are for an intended major including the number of credits the degree program requires. Take at least 25% of those credits each year. Also enroll in the required courses as soon as possible since some of these essential classes may only be available once a year, and even worse, could be a prerequisite for other higher division classes.

If you fall behind, consider summer school at your own college or university or at a community college for general education classes.

Making sure you don't linger unnecessarily will save more than college costs. Graduation delays also keep you from earning a living!

Look for bargains across state lines. If you're eager to attend an out-of-state public school, you won't necessarily have to pay full price. As mentioned earlier in the book, plenty of public universities will discount their out-of-state tuition to desirable kids living beyond their boundaries. The average discount from public universities, according to the College Board, was recently 14.7%.

Here's another way to reduce your costs: Look for out-of-state schools that observe a reciprocity agreement with institutions in your state. Thanks to one of these agreements, you may pay the same price as a resident or capture a significant discount.

Why would a university in Missouri, for instance, extend a price break to a kid from Kansas? Here's one big reason: States decided it was easier to piggyback off the offerings of nearby states than to spend the money developing certain majors on their own. The University of Kansas, for instance, operates an architecture school, but the University of Missouri does not. The University of Missouri system, however, has schools of dentistry and optometry, which KU does not.

Consequently, dentistry and optometry students from Kansas can pay resident tuition at the University of Missouri, while Missouri students can enjoy the same deal when enrolled as architecture students at KU and Kansas State University. Some states have their own reciprocity agreements, but major regional pacts also exist.

Don't expect schools to advertise these bargains—you have to do your own research. You also can't expect all the public schools in a state to be eligible for price discounts. Often the most sought after state schools aren't. Request the reciprocal deal at the same time you apply to a school.

Here are the major regional reciprocal pacts:

- **Academic Common Market (www.sreb.org/programs/acm/acmindex.asp).** Member states: Alabama, Arkansas, Delaware, Florida (graduate programs only), Georgia, Kentucky, Louisiana, Maryland, Mississippi, North Carolina (graduate programs only), Oklahoma, South Carolina, Tennessee, Texas (graduate programs only), Virginia, and West Virginia.

- **Midwestern Higher Education Compact (www.mhec.org).** Member states: Illinois, Indiana, Iowa, Kansas, Michigan, Minnesota, Missouri, Nebraska, North Dakota, Ohio, and Wisconsin.
- **New England Board of Higher Education (www.nebhe.org).** All 78 public colleges and universities participate in the tuition discount program offered in these six states: Connecticut, Maine, Massachusetts, New Hampshire, Rhode Island, and Vermont.
- **Western Undergraduate Exchange (http://wue.wiche.edu/).** Member states: Alaska, Arizona, California, Colorado, Hawaii, Idaho, Montana, Nevada, New Mexico, North Dakota, Oregon, South Dakota, Utah, Washington, and Wyoming.

Start at a community college. Beginning at a community college can save a bundle of money. According to the American Association of Community Colleges, the average community college tuition is $2,272. The trick to starting at a community college is making sure all those credits transfer to four-year institutions later.

Head north. If you want an educational bargain, consider Canadian schools. According to the *Fiske Guide to Colleges*, which covers leading Canadian universities in its annual guide, the typical Canadian student was recently paying just $2,500. Of course, Americans can't expect that price, but the cost could still be lower than out-of-state public universities and private schools.

Many competitive Canadian schools offer merit scholarships to qualified students, regardless of citizenship. You can learn more about Canadian schools by visiting the Web site of the Association of Universities and Colleges of Canada (www.aucc.ca). Another Canadian resource for more than 1,700 colleges and universities is SchoolFinder.com.

Action Plan

- Look for schools that have solid four-year graduation rates, and you'll save yourself a ton of money.
- Check for bargains in nearby states.

41

Shrinking the College Tab, Part II

The person who does not ask will never get a bargain.

—French Proverb

Need more ideas to clip college costs? Here are a few more:

Lean on your kids. Even if you can afford to underwrite all four (or more) years of your child's college career, don't do it. Your child, despite his or her whining, will greatly benefit from paying at least part of the tab. If teenagers haven't spent time cleaning a deep fat fryer at McDonald's or playing Candyland for the umpteenth time at a babysitting gig, it can be difficult for them to appreciate how hard people have to work for their money.

If they enter college still thinking that money is imbued with magical properties—it just appears when needed—they could ultimately have a much tougher time dealing with the realities of the working world. And before that milestone, they may have more trouble buckling down at school because they don't own a financial stake in their education.

It's important to talk with your child long before the freshman year is looming about how much money he or she must contribute to his or her college education. You might decide that she has to pay for certain expenses, such as textbooks and living expenses. Another idea is for your child to kick in the equivalent of what she can borrow yearly through the federal Stafford loans, which are designed for students.

On many, if not most, campuses it's easy for students to find work. According to the American Council on Education, anywhere from

70% to 80% of college students work. Holding a part-time job not only defrays costs, but it can also boost your child's grade point average. Studies show that kids who work part time typically enjoy higher grades than those who don't. Juggling school and work commitments is an excellent skill to develop for a future career.

Check out nonprofit lenders. Some nonprofit lenders, which are often state chartered, provide great deals for certain students, such as those selecting particular majors. These lenders, for instance, may shrink interest rates for students who choose public service fields or nursing in states where there is a desperate need for young people. For instance, Missouri residents who want to go into law enforcement, social work, and other public service careers could recently borrow money from the Missouri Higher Education Loan Authority (MOHELA) for an infinitesimal .5% interest rate. That's right, a half percent. The Michigan Higher Education Student Loan Authority was recently offering engineering students in the state—residents and nonresidents—a great deal. If they met certain qualifications, engineering students could capture a 0% interest rate on their federal Stafford loans.

Leave the car at home. Many colleges prefer that students, particularly underclassmen, keep their cars at home. You can save a nice chunk of change by dry-docking your kid's car. Obviously, the gas bill disappears and the maintenance costs should shrivel too. What's more, you may be able to freeze the insurance payments until your child returns home.

Even if your son or daughter doesn't own a car, you should still contact your insurer when he or she leaves in the fall. Insurers could slash the price of your child's coverage or eliminate the cost entirely until he or she starts driving again. To obtain price breaks or even bill moratoriums, some insurers require that the child's school be more than 100 miles away from home.

Admittedly, it might not be much of a consolation to a child without a car, but walking or riding a bike is a lot healthier and can help your child avoid the "freshman 15." That's the number of pounds new college students are thought to gain.

Become a residential advisor. If your child is responsible and blessed with good social skills, he or she might want to be an RA. An

RA serves as surrogate mother hen to the kids in a dormitory. RAs help settle disputes and make sure kids aren't doing dumb things like hauling beer kegs into their dorm rooms. Colleges and universities generally reward their RAs, who typically have to be sophomores or upperclassmen, by eliminating or reducing their room and board expenses or tuition.

Collect cheap college credits. Taking college level Advanced Placement courses while in high school can shave a semester or more from your undergraduate career. Another alternative is getting college credits through the College-Level Examination Program (CLEP), which allows students of any age to demonstrate proficiency in college courses. More than 2,900 colleges and universities participate in the CLEP program. High school students can also obtain college credit by taking community college classes in the summer.

Buy used books. According to one federal study, the cost of textbooks has jumped nearly four times the rate of inflation since 1994. Expect to be gouged if you wander into your college's bookstore and buy new textbooks. Buying used books will obviously save money. One handy resource is BestBookBuys.com, which is an online price comparison shopping site that scans prices at many online bookstores. Also see whether your college offers a textbook swapping service. Other sources for used textbooks are BarnesandNoble.com and Amazon.com.

Apply for free. College expenses start adding up even before you enroll. It can cost $60 to $70 a pop just to apply to colleges. A Web site called, Free College Applications, maintains a list of many schools that offer free or reduced-price applications. You can find the site at www.porcelina.net/freeapps/.

Check for discounts. Ask a school whether it grants a discount for a second child who attends the school or for recommending the school to a friend who enrolled. Also inquire whether you can charge the tuition on your credit card to capture frequent flyer miles or other plastic perks.

Action Plan

Students should pay a portion of their college costs. Having a part-time job can actually improve a student's grades.

42

Freebies and Best Buys

The best things in life are free.

—American proverb

While parents shudder at the cost of a higher education today, a handful of colleges scattered across the country charge less tuition than a bag of theater popcorn. Yes, they are free. Even better, some of these generous schools don't charge for room and board either.

Some of the places that waive the tuition costs are so-called working colleges, while other schools don't require their students to lift a finger. Some of the most magnanimous colleges are also among the most elite, even though most families have probably never heard of them. The first three schools definitely fit that description. All three waive tuition, and the last school on the list also waives room and board:

Franklin W. Olin College of Engineering, Needham, Massachusetts. This college graduated its first class in 2006, but its reputation is spreading fast among bright students who aspire to be engineers. The F.W. Olin Foundation underwrites the tiny school, which has just more than 300 students. The admission process is unique because it invites about 180 finalists to the campus to participate in a design project, team exercises, and interviews. Academic slouches aren't welcome at this school. The 79 students in the class of 2011 include 39 National Merit Scholarship finalists and 15 valedictorians.

The Cooper Union for the Advancement of Science and Art, New York City. This is another highly desirable destination for engineering students, as well as architects and artists. Actually, the school, which was founded in 1859, offers bachelor's degrees in all three areas. About 900 students attend this school, which was founded by Peter Cooper, an industrialist and inventor, who had less than one year of formal schooling. Thomas Edison attended Cooper Union, and the Red Cross and NAACP were organized here.

Deep Springs College, Deep Springs, California. This college, plunked down on a working cattle ranch and alfalfa farm in a parched desert near the Nevada state line, is an oddity for more than its location. It's a two-year college that attracts brilliant male students (women aren't allowed) who have typically graduated at the very top of their high schools. The school caps enrollment at 26 students. The teenagers who are accepted have earned close to a perfect SAT critical reading score of 800, as well as extremely high math scores. After spending two years in the desert, students head off to prestigious institutions, including the Ivies.

Working Colleges

Working colleges represent another source of free tuition or significantly reduced fees. Everyone holds a job at these colleges, which integrate work with academics. While there were hundreds of these colleges in the mid nineteenth century, today only seven schools meet the federal definition of a working college. Kids work on campus farms, repair computers, work at daycare centers for the community, and operate dining halls. The vast majority of students work at least 140 hours per semester.

These three working schools do not charge tuition:

Berea College, Berea, Kentucky. Started by an abolitionist in the mid 1800s as the South's first interracial and coeducational college, Berea College reaches out to promising students who couldn't go to college without a helping hand. The school estimates that the cost of the education exceeds $23,000 a year. The school's admission hurdle isn't insurmountable. The average ACT score—the ACT rather than the SAT is commonly used in the South and Midwest—was 23.6. The free offer attracts so many applicants that the acceptance rate is 29%.

College of the Ozarks, Point Lookout, Missouri. This school calls itself Hard Work U. The academic requirements for admission aren't strenuous. The middle range is 21 to 26 on the ACT, but the school's popularity has kept its acceptance rate of just 12% comparable to Ivy League schools. Students are expected to work 15 hours a week on campus, as well as two 40-hour weeks when school isn't in session.

Alice Lloyd College, Pippa Passes, Kentucky. This school has bragged that it was cited by *U.S. News & World Report* as the No. 1 private school where graduates leave with the least amount of debt. The school's tuition is waived for students who live in a 108-county area of Appalachia that crosses into five states. About 96% of graduates either have a job or are enrolled in graduate school six months after they've left Alice Lloyd.

Here are the remaining working colleges:

Blackburn College, Carlinville, Illinois
Ecclesia College, Springdale, Arkansas
Sterling College, Craftsbury Common, Vermont
Warren Wilson College, Asheville, North Carolina

In addition, Knoxville College in Knoxville, Tennessee, which was involved in a working program until the late 1920s, is actively seeking to revive it. Berry College in Mount Berry, Georgia, shares many of the traits of a working college.

To learn more about working colleges visit the Web site of the Work Colleges Consortium (www.workcolleges.org).

Blue Light Specials

Although there aren't many colleges that let you attend for free, a handful of other colleges and universities have slashed their sticker price for all students. Bethany College in Bethany, West Virginia, shrank its tuition by 42% a few years ago, while North Park University in Chicago cut its tuition by 30%. The University of South Dakota, which is in a state that's experiencing a troubling drop in population, halved its tuition for out-of-state students. Recently, the university was charging outsiders $6,631 for tuition, which is only about $1,200 more than the locals. Other schools that dramatically cut their tuition include the College of Idaho in Caldwell, Idaho, Muskingum College in New Concord, Ohio, and Wells College in Aurora, New York.

From a marketing standpoint, taking this approach, although beneficial to students, can be risky. Parents and kids are naturally going to wonder why a school is willing to educate students for far less money. Are they really hard up for kids to fill the desks?

Actually, lowering the sticker price can simultaneously boost a college's fortunes and help its students. When the cost drops, a college doesn't have to give as large a handout to needy students or as many tuition discounts to more affluent students. This can ultimately leave a school with more money for its operations.

Graduation Guarantees

Another way to shrink costs is to look for schools that guarantee students will graduate in four years. If students follow certain guidelines and can't make it out in four years, the following schools provide the remaining classes at no charge:

Augsburg College, Minneapolis, Minnesota
Centre College, Danfield, Kentucky
DePauw University, Greencastle, Indiana
Doane College, Crete, Nebraska
Dominican University of California, San Rafael, California
Juniata College, Huntingdon, Pennsylvania

Milwaukee School of Engineering, Milwaukee, Wisconsin
Muskingum College, New Concord, Ohio
Pace University, New York City
Regis University, Denver, Colorado
University of Pacific, Stockton, California

Action Plan

If inexpensive or free colleges sounds appealing, consider giving them a serious look.

43

Capturing Private Scholarships

You cannot make footprints in the sands of time while sitting on the beach.

—Nelson Rockefeller, former U.S. vice president and governor

If you're motivated, billions of dollars in private scholarships are waiting for you to chase after them. Luckily, all this money isn't just reserved for the egghead kid who will eventually have to decide whether he or she will turn down the admission offer from Harvard or Yale. Plenty of regular kids can earn them too. But ultimately, only about 7% of students win one.

Before learning more about private scholarships, however, you need to appreciate some of the harsh realities about these prizes. Private scholarships are often only awarded for one year. So if you work really hard to win scholarships to cover your freshman year, you will still have to deal with three years of colleges costs.

But here is what can be most discouraging: Enterprising students who capture a scholarship can jeopardize a portion of their financial aid award. Federal rules require that a school consider outside scholarship money when calculating its financial aid package. Let's say, for instance, that a family's expected contribution to a school is $15,000 and the cost of the college is $25,000. The school offers a financial aid package of $10,000 to fill the gap. Now let's suppose that the student wins a $2,000 scholarship. The school would reduce its financial aid package by $2,000.

When this occurs, it's better if a college reduces the size of a loan in a package rather than grant money that needn't be repaid. Some schools will and some won't. It makes sense to ask financial aid officers at the institutions that interest you about their policies regarding private scholarships.

Frankly, it will often be more worthwhile for students to look for merit awards from individual schools. The school scholarships are often far more lucrative than what you can expect with a private scholarship, and they typically last four years. A study conducted by the Institute for Higher Education Policy concluded that the average private scholarship for undergraduates is worth $1,982.

Finding Private Scholarships

Typically, the best known scholarships are also going to be the hardest to win. Brilliant kids who have the most remarkable resumes are going to snag national scholarships such as the Coca-Cola Scholars awards, the AXA Achievement Scholarship, Gates Millennium Scholars, and the Intel Science Talent Search. Most of the kids who contemplate applying for these sorts of mega awards will be wasting their time.

So what about everybody else? Here's the best way for a child to proceed:

Aim lower. Find loose scholarship cash by hunting in your own community and region. Do your parents' workplaces offer scholarships to children of employees? Some unions also kick in money for the right kid. Service organizations are another good vein to mine. Here are some to contact:

- Lions Club
- Kiwanis International
- Rotary Clubs
- Independent Order of Odd Fellows and Rebekah Lodges
- Benevolent & Protective Order of Elks
- Optimist International
- Soroptimist International

Community foundations are overlooked local resources. These local foundations—there are more than 650 scattered across the country—play matchmaker between generous benefactors in an area and deserving charitable projects. Contact the nearest community foundation to see whether it operates scholarship programs. To find them, visit the community foundation locator sponsored by the Council on Foundations and the Community Foundations of America at www.communityfoundations.net.

Also check for scholarship treasures in your high school's guidance department. Periodically ask the counselor for any new scholarship possibilities. Visit the resource desk at the local library.

The most successful treasure hunters will be the ones who approach the scholarship process as a part-time job. Finding scholarships, filling out applications, and writing essays can ultimately be more lucrative than a job at Baskin-Robbins.

Explore free online scholarship tools. Online scholarship locators will simplify your job. Once at the free sites, you can personalize your search by typing in your interests, accomplishments, and other unique aspects about yourself. The database will compare your profile with the requirements of countless scholarships and spit out a list of possibilities. To generate more leads, vary the information you supply on different attempts.

Here are three prominent scholarships search sites:

- **Fast Web**, www.fastweb.com
- **College Board's Scholarship Search**, http://apps.collegeboard.com/cbsearch_ss/welcome.jsp
- **Scholarships.com**, www.scholarships.com

Check for oddball scholarships. Are you left handed? Juniata College in Huntingdon, Pennsylvania, will award up to $1,000 to left-handed students through its Frederick and Mary F. Beckley Scholarship. Loyola University in Chicago offers an incredible deal to students who are Catholic and have a last name of Zolp. A lucky Zolp, sounds like a Dr. Seuss character, will receive free tuition for four years. That's not the only surname scholarship. Texas A&M University bestows a full-ride scholarship to any student with the last name of Scarpinato. Harvard oversees a bunch of surname scholarships.

It's unlikely you can think of any activity—impressive or not—that can't lay claim to its own scholarships. At DePauw University, female music majors who can sing or play "The Star Spangled Banner" with sincerity are eligible for the Icy Frost Bridge Scholarship. The teenage couple who creates the neatest prom outfits that are held together with Duck Brand Duct Tape wins a big scholarship. Ursinus College in Collegeville, Pennsylvania, bestows its J.D. Salinger Award to creative writers who are oddball geniuses. Also in line for free cash from various scholarship sponsors are surfers, golf caddies, twins, vegetarians, duck callers, bowlers, pagans, and kids who can bake incredible apple pies.

Check with the college. Colleges routinely dispense scholarships that alumni or other supporters of the school have established, in some cases decades ago. You shouldn't confuse these scholarships with merit awards that a college or university may automatically bestow if an incoming student meets certain academic criteria. Schools, for instance, may be sitting on pots of money for kids who have devoted hundreds of hours to community service or for students who want to major in languages and study overseas. Many colleges and universities post these scholarship opportunities on their Web sites, but it can pay off to also contact the schools.

Beware of scholarship rip-offs. A ripe breeding ground for rip-off artists are free college financial seminars. Legitimate professionals won't promise that your child will win a scholarship or grant. Be skeptical of any testimonials that you hear from audience members. They could easily be planted in the room to generate sales.

How do you know if you are dealing with a shyster? According to the Federal Trade Commission, here are some of their telltale promises:

- The scholarship is guaranteed or you'll get your money back.
- You can't get this information anywhere else.
- I just need your credit card or bank account number to hold this scholarship.
- The scholarship will cost money.
- You're a finalist in a contest that you never entered.

Learn more about scholarship scams at the Federal Trade Commission's Web site at www.ftc.gov/scholarshipscams. To file a complaint with the FTC call (877) FTC-HELP. Other contacts, if you suspect a scam, are the local Better Business Bureau and your state's department of consumer protection.

Action Plan

Unless your child is a stellar standout, focus on regional or local scholarships. Typically these outside scholarships won't be as lucrative as merit awards that schools distribute.

Part IX

Navigating the Student Loan Maze

44

The Student Loan Fiasco

Recent investigations have exposed disturbing conflicts of interest between student loan companies and some universities or their employees, undermining both the real and perceived integrity of the financial aid process as a whole. College officials have received gifts, trips, stock options, and other benefits from lenders, while some colleges have agreed to recommend certain lenders if those lenders share the proceeds. In other cases, lenders provide staffing or call centers for a campus, posing as college representatives while answering students' questions about financial aid, including loans.

—Project on Student Debt

Can you imagine ripping off a student for a piece of cake? Or maybe a candy bar or a handful of popcorn? In 2007, the student newspaper at the University of Texas broke the story that its financial aid office was using treats as a criterion for the lenders that the school endorsed.

The staffers in the financial aid office pigged out on free barbecue lunches, after-work cocktails, lasagna, cupcakes, and other goodies that competing lenders provided. Jenny Craig isn't the only one who would have disapproved. The office workers seemed more keen on filling their own stomachs than finding the best, most competitive lenders to place on their preferred lender list.

The dubious behavior didn't stop with ice cream and barbecue beef. The university's director of financial aid was fired after it was discovered that he had financial ties to a student loan company that the school was recommending.

Unfortunately, the Lone Star imbroglio is hardly a fluke. Investigations into what's really going on in financial aid cubicles across the country have uncovered other appalling business practices.

How financial aid offices behave is critical because millions of college kids and their families can't pay for a college education without loans. Families borrow roughly $85 billion a year for college, and this captive audience has attracted lenders who want to play financial hardball.

Some families began realizing they were being played for patsies when an upstart lender, My Rich Uncle (www.myrichuncle.com), took out newspaper ads in 2006 that accused some colleges of accepting "payola" and "kickbacks." The schools that engaged in this unscrupulous activity would pocket the money or various perks after agreeing to put the bribing lenders on their preferred lending lists and to bar students from borrowing through competitors. Lenders are extremely eager to land on a school's preferred lists because families rely heavily on them when selecting loans. The lists are supposed to contain loan companies that will provide the best terms and rates for students.

Ultimately, the New York Attorney General's office and others began investigating, which led to a better picture of what was happening. Here are some of the shenanigans that investigators uncovered:

College administrators were serving on lender boards of directors and getting paid for their time. In even more extreme cases, lenders paved the way for college officials to buy shares of their stock at cheap prices that were later cashed in for tremendous profits.

There was also lots of nickel and dime stuff. Lenders rewarded aid officers with tickets to the Rose Bowl and other sporting events. One bank memo uncovered during an investigation by U.S. Sen. Edward M. Kennedy, chair of the Senate's education committee, suggested employees bring a massage therapist to financial aid offices to provide five-minute massages. The same bank suggested that all-female offices would love complimentary pedicures and manicures.

In some cases, schools endorsed lenders and in return the schools received a percentage of loan profits. Here's how the arrangement still works: A lender hands a school a large pot of money to lend to students who wouldn't otherwise qualify for loans because of credit problems. These are sometimes called opportunity pools. In return, the college recommends the lender for its preferred list.

College officials, who participate in this cozy arrangement, argue that the schools don't benefit from this influx of dollars, needy students do. But their spin leaves out some troubling details. When a college puts a lender on a preferred list in exchange for extra student loan funds, the question that seems to be lost in this transaction is this: Is this lender offering the best deals for the students? If not, the students and their parents are getting saddled with inferior loans just so the school can grab some extra cash.

And the questions don't end there. The money in these opportunity pools are private loans, which, as you'll soon learn, are the worst type of debt. The interest rate on these loans is rarely capped, and there are few consumer protections.

These incestuous, hidden relationships extend beyond placing lenders on preferred lists and making it difficult for students to look elsewhere for loans. At some schools, financial institutions have manned campus call centers that field inquiries from students asking questions about financial aid. In many cases, students have no idea that a lender, rather than a school financial aid officer, is providing the advice.

Lenders don't seem to have overlooked any opportunity to reel in potential customers, which is why lenders are just as interested in students when they are on the verge of graduating. At some schools, for instance, graduating seniors are required to attend an information session that discusses loan consolidation and other concerns that could be relevant to new graduates. In fact, some schools won't allow students to graduate until they sit in on a session. What these kids could be attending, however, is a thinly disguised infomercial.

It is not hard to figure out why lenders want to talk with departing graduates. The industry makes money on consolidating the debt that students have accumulated over several years.

Obviously, the behavior mentioned in this chapter is despicable. Some of the culprits have cleaned up their act, but others haven't. If you must borrow money to pay the college tab—and most families do—you'll learn how to protect yourself in the next four chapters.

Action Plan

Unfortunately, you can't assume that a school will always make the best recommendations for families who need to borrow money. Remain skeptical.

45

Student Loan Primer

Our parents always told us that hard work was the only road to success, but if they're so "successful" why are we stuck with all these student loans?

—Wake Forest University student, CollegeHumor.com

In the summer of 2007, the U.S. Department of Education sent letters to 721 colleges, universities, and trade schools where student lending practices seemed fishy. The government determined that the source of most of the student loans at each of these schools came from one lucky lender. At all these schools, a solitary lender held at least 80% of the institution's federal student loan volume. On some campuses, a single lender presided over a monopoly.

Because many lenders are eager to provide loans to college kids, you've got to wonder why any school would allow one competitor to dominate. Some schools explained that one lender was clearly the superior choice, so its students gravitated to it. But the discovery sure seemed to mock the notion of comparison shopping.

In its letter, the federal government didn't accuse the schools of lawbreaking, but the list did inflame the worst fears of student loan industry critics who have watched one school after another get caught with its hand in the cookie jar. As mentioned in Chapter 44, "The Student Loan Fiasco," investigations have revealed that some colleges and universities—no one knows the exact number—have been selling out their student and parent borrowers for their own gain.

If you must borrow, there are proven ways to cut your costs. Just as important, you've got to know which loans are worth pursuing. Here's what you need to understand to protect yourself:

Use federal loans first. Federal loans are the superior choice for families. Unlike private loans, federal loans offer lower interest rates and fixed monthly payments. What's more, federal loans offer repayment plans based on a graduate's income, deferments for financial hardships, and cancellation provisions if the borrower dies or becomes totally and permanently disabled.

Here are the main federal loans:

Stafford loans. These loans come in two flavors—subsidized and unsubsidized. The subsidized Stafford, reserved for needier students, is more attractive because the government pays the interest while the student remains in school. To get an idea of who qualifies, about two-thirds of students with subsidized loans have adjusted family incomes of less than $50,000, while a quarter of students have family incomes up to $100,000. Less than 10% of students with subsidized Staffords have family incomes that exceed $100,000. In contrast, the unsubsidized Stafford is available to students regardless of their parents' income.

Unfortunately, many families won't be able to borrow all that they need through a Stafford loan. The government has received a lot of flak for maintaining a low Stafford borrowing ceiling. Most freshmen and sophomores can only borrow up to $3,500 and $4,500, respectively, while juniors and seniors can obtain $5,500 each year.

PLUS loans. While Staffords are reserved for student borrowers, the Parent PLUS loan, which is also federally backed, is designed for moms and dads. Parents can borrow enough to meet the cost of a school's attendance that isn't covered by their child's financial aid package. Unlike a Stafford, there is no set borrowing limit. While Stafford loans provide a grace period before payments are required, parents must start repaying the PLUS debt up to 60 days after the loan is fully dispersed.

Parents who own homes should compare the fixed rate of a PLUS, along with its fees, with another alternative—a home equity line of credit. They also need to plug potential tax breaks into this equation. Parents can deduct home equity interest off their taxes if they itemize, but they may also qualify for an above-the-line tax deduction for college loan interest even if they don't itemize.

For parents who don't own a home or who have little home equity, the PLUS Loan is a no-brainer compared to signing a private loan, which should be your last resort.

Let students borrow first. Even if parents intend to borrow for college, it's always better for the student to take out a federal loan in his or her own name first. Why? Stafford loans offer a lower interest rate than the federal PLUS loans. The maximum rate for a Stafford was recently 6.8% versus 8.5% for a PLUS. Beginning in the summer of 2008, the rate became even lower for *subsidized* Staffords and the interest rates will continue to shrink for these undergraduate borrowers.

TABLE 45.1 Interest Rate Reductions for Subsidized Stafford Loans

First Disbursement of a Loan Made On or After	Interest Rate on the Unpaid Balance
July 1, 2008	6.0%
July 1, 2009	5.6%
July 1, 2010	4.5%
July 1, 2011	3.4%

Although your son or daughter is responsible for the payments, you can reimburse the child. Young college graduates are more likely than their parents to be eligible to deduct student loan interest off their yearly income tax returns.

Look beyond the preferred list. To make shopping for loans more manageable, many schools compile a list of preferred lenders. A school could maintain a list of lenders for Stafford loans, PLUS loans, private loans, and consolidation loans. Colleges are expected to select lenders for these lists that offer students the best deals on interest rates and/or customer service or other factors.

By now, you can probably appreciate why you shouldn't automatically assume that these preferred lists are stuffed with tremendous deals. Ask a school's financial aid administrator why lenders made the cut and use these names only as a starting point since you can borrow from any lender. You'll want to ask about interest rates, fees, customer service, and any interest rate discounts. As of July 2008, federal regulations began requiring that colleges put at least three lenders on their preferred lists.

Understand federal loan differences. Not all colleges generate preferred lists because they participate in a direct federal loan program. About 20% of schools offer their students federal guaranteed loans directly from the U.S. Department of Education through the Federal Direct Student Loan Program. All other students receive federally guaranteed loans through private lenders via the Federal Family Education Loan Program.

Your choice will be easy if the school you attend participates only in the federal direct loan program. At these schools, there is one loan option, which is the same for everybody who borrows this way. (About 30% of direct loan schools also participate in Federal Family Education Loan Program.) In the early days of the direct lending program, many more schools participated, and this competition worried the private lenders. To protect their territory, the outside lenders began offering perks to schools to encourage them to shun the direct program, and it worked. If a school is in the FFEL program, its students can borrow money from countless financial institutions that participate in the program.

Direct loans became available in the 1990s when President Bill Clinton and others concluded that it would save taxpayers a lot of money if the government lent the cash to students without a middle man. It costs the government more when students borrow from outside lenders, but obviously families are worried about their own costs, not the federal government's financial problems.

Many students might prefer sticking with direct federal loans for a compelling reason: Only direct loans provide a financial safety valve that allows borrowers who choose lower-paying careers to make monthly payments based on their income, which can be worth its weight in gold.

What's more, a feature called the *income-contingent repayment* allows the monthly payments to be calculated based on the size of the loan, as well as the former student's salary and family size. These loans can't drag on for more than 25 years because if they haven't been paid off by then, the debt is canceled. If debt is forgiven, you will owe income taxes on the forgiven amount, but that's obviously a long way off.

As of July 2009, however, borrowers of Stafford loans and Grad PLUS loans, which are strictly for graduate students, can also choose a newer feature called income-based repayments. While it's similar to the income-contingent plan, the new alternative results in lower monthly payments. By choosing income-based repayments, borrowers will limit their repayments to 15% of their yearly discretionary income, which is defined as the amount by which adjusted gross income exceeds 150% of the poverty line. What's more, direct loan borrowers who work full time for at least a decade in public service jobs, will have their loan forgiven after paying it off for 10 years. Other borrowers can qualify for public service loan forgiveness by consolidating their loans into the direct loan program.

While outside lenders can offer income-based repayments, it's unclear how many of them will. If a private lender doesn't, however, a borrower is entitled to obtain a federal direct consolidation loan on the grounds that his or her lender didn't provide the new feature.

Evaluate repayment plans. Student loans typically offer a handful of alternatives to repay the debt. The traditional way requires a borrower to begin writing checks that cover the loan's principal and interest right after the loan has been made. You can usually capture the lowest interest rates with this option.

Another alternative is simply making interest payments until after graduation. Borrowers who are saddled with the higher rates and fees are those who delay paying anything until they've graduated. The monthly payments will also be higher because the unpaid interest that's been accruing will be dumped back into the loan.

Be realistic. This may sound cruel, but if you aspire to be a social worker or a painter, you probably shouldn't borrow as much as a future dermatologist or investment banker. Here's a handy rule of thumb: Don't borrow more than your anticipated starting salary after you graduate. If you borrow more than twice your starting salary, it's likely you will be in extreme financial difficulty and will struggle to make the monthly payments. Borrowing too much for an education can be even more perilous for students who end up in trade schools.

Action Plan

Always choose federal loans first and avoid private loans.

46

Disappearing Discounts

All else being equal, discounts which require a shorter delay until the borrower qualifies are better than those which require a longer delay.

—Mark Kantrowitz, publisher of FinAid.org

Suppose a lender offers you a student loan with a future interest rate cut of 2%. The lender promises that if you make your payments on time for 48 months, it will slash your rate by two percentage points. What a deal.

Or is it?

Lenders like to tantalize students with rate cuts to capture their business, but too many of these discounts end up being worth less than a Snickers bar.

Lending institutions originally trotted out student loan discounts to make their deals look better than the plain vanilla direct loans that come straight from the federal government. Private lenders now also use them to compete against each other.

You will commonly see lenders offer discounts on federal loans that, by law, set a maximum interest rate ceiling. Recently, for instance, the maximum interest rate on a Stafford loan was 6.8%. Nobody is stopping lenders from charging less than 6.8%, and often they do this through discounts.

Families love discounts, but they need to know that they aren't always the beneficiary of these price slashes. Let's take a look at a discount that has attracted a lot of students. Borrowers signed onto loans that offered a 2% interest rate discount that kicked in if they made 48 months of consecutive payments. Guess what happens, however, if the student forgets to put a stamp on the envelope or forgets to sign his name on the check or for some other reason fails to make the monthly payment one lousy time? The discount vaporizes.

In reality, almost all students trip up on the 48-month hurdle. Mark Kantrowitz, the founder of FinAid.org, estimates that only about 3% of students have managed to earn that tantalizing 2% discount in full. And it gets worse: For the lucky students who do snag the price break, their rate reduction will only pencil out to .63% since the loan will already be four years old before the discount is activated. A 1% discount that requires four years of timely payments, according to Kantrowitz, would ultimately be worth .32%.

What discounts are the best? Look for loans offering upfront discounts. Many lenders, for instance, give borrowers a discount for paying their loans each month through automatic bank debits. If you choose to pay this way, you can typically expect a rate discount of .25%. Paying automatically also boosts your chances of never missing a monthly deadline. Other desirable discounts include fee rebates that kick in shortly after you sign the loan documents, as well as reductions in the loan's principal or rate that don't hinge on timely payments.

There is no need to compare these tricky discounts by yourself. Let someone else do the math by using FinAid's Loan Discount Analyzer (www.finaid.org/calculators).

Action Plan

Always ask whether a loan comes with a discount. Upfront discounts are superior to those that impose a waiting period.

47

Private Loan Perils

Nearly 50% of undergraduate private student loan borrowers fail to exhaust their low-cost federal student loans to finance their college education.

—Consumers Union report

Alison Rabil, the director of financial aid at Barnard College, became concerned one day when she was examining figures on the number of students at the women's college who were taking out private loans.

Rabil and others in Barnard's financial aid office certainly understood why private loans should be a last resort. But the school's parents, even though many were college educated, didn't appreciate the potential hazards of a private loan, which is the fastest growing source of student debt in the country.

Consequently, the school in New York City decided to educate its moms and dads. When Barnard learns that a family is on the verge of assuming a private loan, the school arranges a phone interview with parents. After conversations with Barnard staffers, families often abandon their plan to rely on a private loan. Thanks to Barnard's initiative, according to *Inside Higher Ed*, an online industry publication, the volume of private loans at the school plummeted by 73%.

If you're not sure why private loans should be a last resort, keep reading. Here is what you need to know:

Private loans charge variable interest rates. Anyone with an adjustable rate mortgage already knows why loans without ceiling caps can be perilous. A loan with runaway payments can wreak havoc on a student's or parents' budget. Many people don't realize that private loan payments, which might initially seem manageable, will change because most private loans include variable interest rates that lack a ceiling cap.

Private lenders can discriminate. Unlike federal loan programs, lenders that market private loans can pick and choose their customers. Families with excellent credit can obtain better starting interest rates than those with average or worse credit histories. The less fortunate borrowers can get saddled with loans as bad as the subprime mortgages that helped smash the housing bubble. The spread between the starting interest rate for stellar customers versus those stuck with the worst rate can be 10 percentage points or more.

What's more, the interest rates and fees of private loans can vary from school to school. Some lenders take into account a school's overall loan default rate. So even if you have a pristine credit history, you could still get punished.

Private loans can be confusing. Many families who end up with a private loan believe they have secured a federal loan. Sometimes they don't even realize the mistake they made until they try to consolidate the debt with federal loans. There are many reasons for the confusion. First, the loan process can be bewildering. And families, after surviving the college matchmaking process, may hardly be in the mood to sort through loan possibilities in the spring and summer leading up to a child's freshman year.

Parents and students just want the cash, and they figure they'll worry about how to pay it back later.

If you're considering a private loan, here is what you should be doing:

Use federal loans first. Families should not consider private loans, which are also called alternative loans, unless they have maxed out the federal loans, which offer better terms and more flexible repayment options. Federally guaranteed loans provide fixed rates, and everybody—regardless of their FICO credit scores—receives the same fixed interest rates.

The subsidized and unsubsidized federal Stafford loans are better alternatives for student borrowers and the PLUS loan is best for parents. If you meet the income qualifications, the federal Perkins Loan is the cheapest.

Many families, however, are routinely snubbing federal assistance. According to the Institute for Higher Education Policy, an astounding 20% of dependent students who have private loans never took advantage of federal loans. Another 19% of borrowers never maxed out their federal loans before embracing the private alternative.

Sadly, there are not enough schools like Barnard that are educating parents about the perils of private loans. Some might assume that Barnard can conduct its education effort because it's small, but Colorado State University has proven that even major institutions can spread the word. At Colorado State, about 20% of applicants for private loans either fail to exhaust their federal loan eligibility or skip filing the FAFSA, which is a requirement for obtaining federal loans. Staffers in the financial aid office at Colorado State call every family that falls into one of these two categories and explain their options.

Cosign the loan. Because a borrower's credit record is so important for private loans, students are at a disadvantage when they apply solo. With little or no history of using credit wisely, they can easily get stiffed with mediocre loans that pass along higher interest rates and fees. A parent who has good credit can avoid this problem by taking out the loan themselves or by cosigning the loan. Most lenders will consider only the highest credit scores among co-borrowers. What's more, the interest rate formulas for cosigned loans are slightly better than those on noncosigned loans for the same credit score.

Don't get tricked by slick marketers. If you've got a teenager who will head off to college soon, lenders are probably stuffing your mailbox with junk mail that makes obtaining a private loan seem as easy as ordering Chinese takeout.

Here's an excerpt from a letter sent by Sallie Mae, the big gorilla in the student lending industry, that I received a couple of months before my daughter began college: "Classes will start again before you know it. Don't let worrying about college expenses ruin your summer...Applying is fast, free and easy. Borrow up to $40,000 a year."

Sallie Mae went on to promise that my husband and I wouldn't have to worry about filling out any federal financial aid forms! Many parents might think that is a plus, but the lender was recklessly providing families with a way to jeopardize their chances for the best financial aid. Parents should fill out the federal form—FAFSA—because without doing so, they can't obtain federal loans, which are far preferable.

All the junk mail I received from lenders made private loans seem like the best approach by offering, in the words of one lender, "fast" credit decisions, "quick" renewals, and "easy" online applications. If you haven't been bombarded with these promotions, your child could be getting inundated by Internet pop-up ads touting these loans.

The promises sound great, but the price you pay will be high.

Don't be fooled by branded loans. When students receive their financial aid packages, sometimes they will contain loans that bear the name of the school. Beware of private loans masquerading as school loans that are nothing more than marketing ploys. Students may assume that the school branded loans are more favorable, but these loans typically are just like any other private loan, and in some cases they could be worse.

Ask intelligent questions. Before committing to a private loan, ask these questions:

- Can I get a fixed-rate loan?
- If the interest rate is variable, is there a cap on how high it can go?
- What percentage of borrowers gets the best rate?
- Do you offer an interest rate discount or a reduction in principal if I make on-time payments?
- Does the discount kick in when I start paying off my loan?
- If the discount isn't immediate, how many months of on-time payments must I make?
- If I miss a payment, is there anyway to recapture the discount?
- Are your discounts guaranteed or could they disappear later?
- If I encounter financial hardship, will you allow me to stop payments temporarily without financially penalizing me?
- Is there a prepayment penalty?
- What index are your loans tied to?

Check your credit. If you're contemplating applying for a private loan, check your credit report. By federal law, you are entitled to a free credit report annually from each of the three major credit bureaus:

Equifax (800) 685-1111, www.equifax.com

Experian (888) 397-3742, www.experian.com

TransUnion (800) 888-4213, www.transunion.com

If something is wrong, you'll want to correct it.

Unfortunately, what the free reports can't tell you is your credit score. FICO, which is an abbreviation for its creator, Fair Isaac Corporation, is the most common credit score. FICO scores range from 300 (abysmal) to 850 (phenomenal). Financial institutions generally require minimum scores of 700 to 720 to qualify for the best loan interest rates and terms. About 58% of Americans recently managed to have a FICO score that was at least 700.

If your FICO score is less than 620 to 650, you will generally not qualify for private student loans. Most lenders have five or six credit tiers from 650 to 850 so a 30- to 40-point change in a credit score can have a big impact on the cost of a loan.

If your credit score isn't great, you should definitely try boosting it. Taking this initiative could ultimately save you thousands of dollars if you qualify for a more attractive private loan. You can discover many ways to do just that by reading an excellent book, *Your Credit Score: How to Fix, Improve, and Protect the 3-Digit Number that Shapes Your Financial Future*, 2nd edition, by Liz Pulliam Weston.

Make timely payments. You never want to court trouble with a lender whether it's a private institution or the federal government. One of the best ways to avoid punitive penalties for missing payments is to sign up for automatic payments through your checking or savings account. Many people mess up when they change residences and fail to receive their bill. Don't expect lenders to be sympathetic.

Action Plan

Never choose a private loan unless you have maxed out your federal loans.

48

Default Debacles

Student loans are more predatory than payday loans.

—Alan Collinge, founder of StudentLoanJustice.Org

When Alan Collinge left his job as an associate scientist at the California Institute of Technology in 2001, he had no idea of the financial nightmare that awaited him. His next job vanished after September 11, and the young man was forced to struggle on low-paying jobs for a lengthy stretch.

Collinge asked his student lender for a temporary forbearance. A forbearance allows a borrower to temporarily postpone or reduce payments on a loan while the interest continues accruing. Forbearances, as well as loan deferments, are typically given to those who are experiencing economic hardship. Collinge's lender, however, rejected his request and declared the loan in default.

Now here's the mind-blowing part: Thanks to punitive fees and penalties that are commonplace in the student loan industry, Collinge's $38,000 debt that he accumulated as an engineering student at the University of Southern California in the late 1990s ballooned to more than $100,000 by 2007.

The experience prompted Collinge to found StudentLoanJustice.Org, a student lending activist organization, which aims to spread the word about the dangers of student loans and to fight for changes.

Collinge's Web site is full of horrific stories of college graduates and parents whose financial and emotional lives have been ruined by student debt. He's even heard from borrowers who have fled the country or headed underground. Some have committed suicide.

If you're tempted to miss a few payments on your student loan, spend 15 minutes reading some of the heart-wrenching stories on this site. Those who are struggling with their student debt should also visit a new Web site, Student Loan Borrower Assistance, www.studentloanborrowerassistance.org, which is a program that the National Consumer Law Center launched. The project provides information on the rights and responsibilities of student loan borrowers.

Finally, troubled borrowers should also explore a loan default calculator on FinAid, the financial aid Web site (www.finaid.org/calculators/default.phtml). The software calculates the impact of trying to walk away from a loan.

When unveiling the calculator, Mark Kantrowitz, the creator of FinAid, provided a sobering example of the financial nightmare college debtors can experience. In his example, he looked at what would happen if a borrower defaulted on a $20,000, 10-year loan with a 6.8% interest rate. Normally, the borrower would make monthly payments of about $230 for the loan that would generate $7,619 in interest. But suppose the borrower never made any payments. After snubbing the lender for a year, the late fees, collection costs, and delayed payments would inflate the final bill by nearly 82% and take 19.2 years to repay. If the borrower failed to make payments for four years, the total tab would reach $125,237 for an increase of 353%.

Obscene future payments aren't the only punishment. Lenders can sue borrowers, garnish their wages, and, of course, completely trash their credit record.

How many people can afford all that?

Action Plan

Do whatever you can to avoid defaulting on a student loan.

Part X

Maximizing College Accounts

49

A 529 Primer

I look at them (expensive 529 plans) and think, "Are people out of their minds? Why would they put their money in them?"

—Ilene Malitz, former Georgetown University finance professor

If 529 college savings plans seem confusing, you may feel better after you hear the experience of a Harvard University professor. Or then, maybe you'll feel worse.

During an interview, Susan Dynarski, an associate professor of public policy at Harvard University, once told me that she had to abandon her work on a comparison study of 529 plans. Why? Because she concluded it was too hopeless. The expenses and fees were structured so differently it defied comparisons.

An Ivy League education isn't necessary, however, to conclude that Darwin's survival of the fittest theory doesn't apply to the 529 universe. There are some hideously awful 529 plans that should not be walking the planet. Of course, there are some worthwhile plans in the marketplace too. Which brings us back to the part about 529 plans being confusing.

If your child is already a teenager, knowing how 529 plans work, as well as their potential risks and rewards, is arguably less critical than it is for the parents of a newborn. But even if your child is in high school, you can still benefit. It's never too late to invest for college, and if you already own a 529, you'll need to know the rules about tapping into it without triggering taxes. If you have younger children, it's worth reading about and appreciating what 529 plans offer and understanding which are valuable.

Even if you have absolutely zero interest in 529 plans, they can be handy indirectly. How? Because you can steal investment ideas from them. You'll see how in Chapter 50, "College Investing Cheat Sheet." And you'll learn more about withdrawals in Chapter 51, "The Perils of Cashing Out College Accounts."

Other books delve more deeply into 529 plans, as well as other savings approaches, such as the Coverdell Education Savings Account. This chapter is only intended to share the highlights.

529 Backgrounder

The 529 plan, which gets its name from a section of the Internal Revenue Code, received its start in 1996 thanks to federal legislation. Advocates greeted the 529 plan as a way for parents to stuff money into special accounts that offered an attractive tax advantage, which is even greater today.

The federal government, however, didn't do families any favors when it left many of the details on how the 529 plan would work to individual states. With every state able to run its own program, lobbyists for financial service companies fanned out across the country to wrestle for their own piece of the action. This led to states approving plans, in too many cases, that contained mediocre mutual funds studded with bloated fees.

In fact, if you examine a 529 plan, you will often discover that fees are jammed in tighter than a teenager's backpack. Inside, you might find investment fees, maintenance fees, enrollment fees, and who knows what else. Every state has signed off on its own fee structures, which is why it can be excruciatingly difficult to compare one plan to another.

Not all plans are ugly. Some are quite good, but the trick is finding the ideal one. Before you can learn how to locate the right match, you have to understand why 529 plans can often be worth the hassle.

529 Nuts and Bolts

When you invest money in a 529, it's protected from federal income taxes and almost always state taxes as well. As long as the cash remains inside the account, you don't have to worry about taxes. It's also usually, but not always, a nonissue once you begin spending the money on college bills.

When your child enrolls in college, you can pull the cash out and use it for qualified college expenses, such as tuition, room and board, fees, supplies, books, and equipment. You can only use 529 money to pay for a computer if a school requires students to have one. Most states, but not all, allow 529 proceeds to pay for undergraduate and graduate school.

Nearly three dozen states also offer their residents another attractive tax break. These states give 529 savers a full or partial tax deduction on their state income taxes for their contributions. There is, however, a catch. Almost all states require that parents who want to pocket a state tax deduction, choose their own state plan.

The tax breaks range from incredibly generous to barely worth talking about. Five states—Colorado, Illinois, New Mexico, South Carolina, and West Virginia—make the honor roll by letting their residents deduct the full amount of their 529 contributions from their state taxes. Pennsylvania is another magnanimous state. It permits parents to take a tax deduction of up to $12,000 per child, and it doesn't care which state plan they use. Maine, Kansas, and Arizona have also extended their tax break to families that prefer an outside 529.

Don't invest in a 529 just because of your state's tax enticement. Frankly, some state plans are dogs, and tossing in a tax break isn't going to turn them into winners.

If your child will be in college soon, however, you might want to hold your nose and sink some money in a low-risk investment within your state plan—even with mediocre investment choices—if it offers a generous tax deduction.

Advisors Versus Do-It-Yourself

Choosing 529 plans isn't the same as shopping for white socks. While all these plans are dedicated to helping families save for college, the investments and the costs within these programs are wildly different.

Each state has formed alliances with mutual fund families or nationally known brokerage firms to offer investments within each state-sponsored 529. Vanguard, for instance, provides investment options for many state plans, including Nevada, Iowa, Missouri, and New York. If you invest in a 529 in Alaska, you'll get T. Rowe Price mutual funds. Kansas 529 families will invest in American Century, and California and New Hampshire are among the states that use Fidelity Investments. TIAA-CREF manages plans in such states as Michigan, Tennessee, and Connecticut. Some states offer multiple providers.

You can eliminate many plans simply by answering this question: Do I want someone to pick a 529 for me? It's critical to answer this because the plans are divided into two categories. With "direct" plans, you select the state program yourself. In contrast, "advisor" plans require people to invest through an outside professional. States typically offer both types.

The advisor plans tend to be the price hogs because they charge large commissions to compensate the stockbroker or planner who recommended them. Sales charges for 529 purchases used to range from 3% to 3.5% for college savings plans. That ceiling, however, was shattered in 2002 when the state of Virginia created tremendous excitement within the brokerage industry by rolling out a 529 plan offering a 5.75% commission. In response, most state plans increased their commission rates to 5.75%.

The commission, by the way, isn't a one-time occurrence. If you're in an advisor plan, you'll be dinged by the sales charge with each purchase of new 529 shares. It's kind of like continuing to tip the pizza delivery man for years after the pepperoni pizza was delivered.

Check the Costs

Plenty of other rapacious fees can devour your return. You can find a plan's other fees by looking at its program disclosure or program description. A 529 is considered inexpensive if all fees, including the underlying mutual fund costs, pencil out at less than .8% of your investment each year. With that percentage, you'd pay the plan $80 if you had $10,000 in it. Plans that charge between .8% and 1.2% are considered moderately priced. Anything priced higher should be avoided.

Outrageous fees can significantly erode the value of a college fund by the time a child graduates from high school. Assume, for example, that grandparents open a 529 account with $1,000 when their grandchild is born, and they faithfully invest $150 a month for 18 years. Let's also suppose that the 529 generates a yearly return of 8% before expenses. If the grandparents invested in an expensive 529 (2% annual fees), the account would ultimately be worth $61,040. The inexpensive plan (.65% annual fees) would pencil out to $70,831. That's an extra $9,791!

Top 529 Funds

Think cheap and stick with low-cost plans. It's no coincidence that many of the 529 plans that have been feted by the financial press are also the cheapest. Here are some to consider:

- **Utah** (800) 418-2551, www.uesp.org. Underlying funds: Vanguard Group index mutual funds.
- **Nevada** (866) 734-4530, www.vanguard.com. Underlying funds: Vanguard Group index funds.
- **West Virginia** (866) 574-3542, www.smart529.com. Underlying funds: Dimensional Fund Advisors mutual funds.
- **Alaska** (800) 369-3641, www.price529.com. Underlying funds: T. Rowe Price mutual funds.

Prepaid 529 Plan

The 529 savings plan monopolizes the press coverage, but there is another option that fewer states offer—the prepaid 529 plan. Some conservative parents and grandparents who are frightened of Wall Street's occasional tantrums have gravitated to the prepaid plan because it poses no stock market risk.

Prepaid plans, which typically offer a better rate of return than a certificate of deposit, are supposed to grow in value at the same rate as in-state public college tuition. If you bought a year's worth of tuition, for example, it would still be worth that much years later regardless of inflation.

What happens, however, if your child doesn't attend a public school inside his or her state? Suppose a kid has been a Florida State University Seminole fan since he or she was old enough to use the remote control. The family assumed that he or she would attend the school and had saved up enough in the state's prepaid plan to cover the tuition that recently was less than $3,400 a year. But let's imagine that the family moves to Indiana, and the Seminole fan wants to attend Notre Dame or any other school outside Florida. Prepaid plans typically only pay the average of its own public state schools' tuition, or it might refund the money that you sunk into it with or without interest. That amount could obviously be a pittance of what parents need.

There is one notable prepaid source that you won't find on the state level. The Independent 529 Plan (www.independent529plan.org) offers the same sort of prepaid state plan with one significant exception: It won't limit you to schools in one state. This plan is a consortium of hundreds of private colleges and universities that are scattered across the country.

Action Plan

Avoid schlocky 529 plans and stick with the low-cost plans that you can buy directly.

50

College Investing Cheat Sheet

From a financial standpoint, being the parents of college-bound children is no picnic.

—College Board

The toughest part of saving for college is, well, saving. The next toughest part is figuring out where to stash the cash. Investing college money is arguably trickier than saving for retirement because the time horizon is shorter and therefore less forgiving. And that's especially true if your child is in high school.

Obviously, parents can invest far more aggressively if their child is still watching *Sesame Street* rather than borrowing the family car. However, parents who feel paralyzed by an abundance of choices aren't going to find generalities too helpful.

Perhaps the best way to find the answer is to turn to cheat sheets. I'd suggest that you take a look at how some of the major 529 college saving plan providers invest assets for children at different ages. In this chapter, I've included model 529 portfolios that T. Rowe Price and the Vanguard Group offer their college saving clients.

Vanguard and T. Rowe Price, as well as many 529 plan providers, offer age-based investment options that contain a mix of stock and bond mutual funds that grow more conservative as a child ages. You can look at how these sample age-based portfolios invest in stock and bond funds at different stages of a child's life. Perhaps, for example, your child is 14 and you're agonizing over whether you've got too much money allocated to stock in his college fund. If you've got doubts, examine how professional managers are investing for kids that age.

You can use these age-based portfolios, or other ones, as a guide regardless of what type of accounts you own. The breakdown of investment categories can be useful whether you invest in 529 plans, Coverdell Education Savings Accounts, custodial accounts, taxable accounts, or some other way.

The T. Rowe Price portfolios are based on how many years remain before a child enters college. In the Vanguard examples, the model portfolios are based on a range of ages. Naturally, T. Rowe Price uses its own mutual funds in its 529 portfolios, while Vanguard relies on its index mutual funds. The investment breakdowns of 529 plans are contained in their respective program descriptions, which you can obtain by calling the firms or by downloading documents online.

As you'll see there are considerable differences between the portfolios of the two mutual fund giants. What's critical is that you find an investment mix that you will feel comfortable owning.

T. Rowe Price Model Portfolios

College bound students

Bonds	40%
Short-term bonds	40%
Large-cap stocks	20%

Two years until college

Bonds	46%
Short-term bonds	27%
Large-cap stocks	26%
Small-cap stocks	1%

Five years until college

Bonds	50%
Short-term bonds	6%
Large-cap stocks	33%
Mid cap stocks	4%
International stocks	3%

Eight years until college

Bonds	38%
Large-cap stocks	42%
Small-cap stocks	6%
Mid-cap stocks	6%
International stocks	8%

Eleven years until college

Bonds	21%
Large-cap stocks	53%
Small-cap stocks	7%
International stocks	12%
Mid-cap stocks	7%

Fourteen years until college

Bonds	6%
Large-cap stocks	61%
Small-cap stocks	9%
International stocks	15%
Mid-cap stocks	9%

Seventeen years until college

Large-cap stocks	65%
Small-cap stocks	10%
International stocks	15%
Mid-cap stocks	10%

Vanguard's Model Portfolios

Vanguard developed its age-based options for conservative, moderate, and aggressive investors. The moderate age-based portfolio is used in this chapter. All of Vanguard's age-based portfolios use some combination of Vanguard's Total Stock Market Index Fund, Total International Stock Index Fund, Total Bond Market Index Fund, Inflation-Protected Securities Fund, and its Short-Term Reserves Account.

Newborn through age five

Domestic stocks	60%
International stocks	15%
Bonds	25%

Ages six through 10

Domestic stocks	40%
International stocks	10%
Bonds	50%

Ages 11 through 15

Domestic stocks	20%
International stocks	5%
Bonds	75%

Ages 16 and older

Bonds	50%
Inflation-protected securities	25%
Cash	25%

Action Plan

If you're not sure how to divide your college accounts among stock and bond mutual funds, consider using the investment percentages that major mutual fund companies rely on.

51

The Perils of Cashing Out College Accounts

The Internal Revenue Service is the real undefeated heavyweight champion.

—George Foreman, boxing champion

Once your child is enrolled in college, brace yourself. You may have to contend with the Internal Revenue Service's own Rubik's Cube guide to cashing in college accounts. It can be hellish trying to withdraw cash from college accounts without getting hit with taxes or losing valuable tax credits. Frankly, the rules can give you a Slurpee brain freeze.

This chapter can't possibly explore all the permutations of draining various types of college accounts. I could write an entire book on this topic, but a crate of Extra Strength Excedrin couldn't get me to embark on that project. This chapter, however, gives you a taste of what you can expect when you pull out your checkbook.

For parents who understandably want to know more, I'd suggest a couple of resources. The first is free: Visit the Web site of the Internal Revenue Service and obtain the rules from IRS publication 970, "Tax Benefits for Education" (www.irs.gov/pub/irs-pdf/p970.pdf), on how to sidestep these problems.

My other recommendation is to consult a Certified Public Accountant or a financial advisor who really knows these rules. Generalities can only go so far since every family's circumstances vary.

Without further ado, here are some of the preposterous jams you'll want to dodge:

529 Plans That Bite

The reason why so many people gravitate to 529 plans is their celebrated tax benefits. And here's one of the biggies: You don't have to pay Uncle Sam when you withdraw cash from a 529 plan for college.

Unfortunately, some families will discover that this tax reprieve isn't airtight. Parents will owe taxes if the 529 money they withdraw exceeds their so-called qualified higher education expenses. These costs include tuition, mandatory fees, required books, and supplies. If the child is attending school on at least a half-time basis, the room and board is also thrown into the calculation.

If your 529 withdrawals exceed these allowable costs, you'll have to report a portion or all of the account's earnings on your next income tax return. You'd need to use a formula in IRS Publication 970 to determine how much of the earnings would be taxed. And there's more: You could also get hit with a 10% tax penalty.

You might be thinking that it shouldn't be tough to avoid overdrawing a 529 account. But then you would be underestimating the complexity of the tax code. It's the double dipping rules that can trip you up. One of the easiest ways to get into trouble is to use 529 proceeds to pay for college in the same year that you take advantage of the federal Lifetime Learning tax credit.

The Lifetime Learning tax credit provides a family with a maximum $2,000 tax credit, which equals 20% of the first $10,000 paid for tuition and fees. Tax credits, by the way, are fabulous because they knock off dollar for dollar what you owe Uncle Sam in April.

So what's the problem? The government doesn't want you to pocket the Lifetime Learning tax credit for the same expenses (tuition and fees) that you're pulling out of your 529 plan tax free. Here's where the calculations get painful: Let's suppose you withdrew $15,000 from a 529 plan to cover $15,000 in college expenses. So far so good. Then let's suppose you claimed the $2,000 Lifetime

Learning tax credit based on spending $10,000 of that $15,000 in 529 money. That's the no-no.

The government will make you subtract the $10,000, which you relied on to qualify for the maximum Lifetime Learning credit, from your qualified 529 expenses. That would drop your qualified expenses down to $5,000. So as far as the government is concerned, your child's qualified higher ed expenses were only $5,000 even though you paid out more. Consequently, you would be liable for tax on the earnings portion of the other $10,000. If it's any consolation, parents who find themselves in this predicament won't get hit with a 10% withdrawal penalty.

You need to be just as careful when claiming a federal education tax credit—the other one is called the Hope Scholarship tax credit—in the same year that you withdraw money from a Coverdell Education Savings Account. If you use the same expenses for the Coverdell and either tax credit, you will also be guilty of IRS double dipping.

Parents can also trigger taxes if they withdraw too much money when they prepare to pay a January tuition bill. They may pull out 529 money in late December for an expense that won't occur until the next calendar year.

Financial Aid

A lot of parents worry that a 529 will sabotage their hopes for financial aid. If you fall into that category, go ahead and worry about something else. Parents will have to report 529 assets on their federal financial aid forms if they are the account owners of the 529 plans, but the money should have little or no effect on their aid qualification.

If a parent is the primary owner of a 529 account, the 529 account assets are assessed for financial aid purposes at a maximum rate of 5.64%. Here's what that means: For every $10,000 a family has tucked inside a 529 plan, need-based aid would be reduced by $564. That would still leave you with $9,436 more than if you had saved nothing.

Actually, most parents won't see any reduction in aid eligibility. That's because the federal formula gives families an asset protection allowance that generally ranges from $40,000 to $50,000. In other words, the formula ignores that money. The amount depends on the age of the parents—the older you are the higher the allowance. Families can actually shelter more than what's covered by the asset protection allowance. The federal aid formula also doesn't count money inside retirement accounts, the value of a small business owned and controlled by a family, and a family's home.

Thanks to a loophole in federal law—it might be closed by the time you read this—the money in custodial 529 plans isn't considered at all in the federal financial aid need analysis. A custodial 529 can be created when parents take the cash from an UGMA or UTMA custodial account, pay any taxes due, and move the proceeds into a custodial 529. Because the money started in a custodial account, it has to remain in one.

Custodial 529 accounts used to be treated more harshly for financial aid purposes because it was considered a child's asset, but Congressional action changed that. Starting July 1, 2009, custodial 529 plans will be reported as a parent asset if the student is a dependent.

Action Plan

You'll unleash unnecessary taxes if you don't know the rules about withdrawing cash from college accounts.

52

Grading Financial Advisers

Our results demonstrate that 529 plans with higher fees have more accounts and more assets. In this study, investors are choosing out-of-state plans with higher fees and forgoing significant state tax benefits.

—Study conducted by Raquel Meyer Alexander and LeAnn Luna, assistant professors of accounting at the University of Kansas and the University of Tennessee

A few years ago, I was sitting in a corporate auditorium in Michigan listening to a sales rep praise the 529 college savings plan that he was peddling. The rep told the employees in the audience how wonderful 529 plans are and how his 529 plan in particular was first rate. I have no doubt that some of the parents ended up enrolling in this plan. The guy was that convincing.

What I found disturbing about the presentation was what remained unsaid. The speaker never mentioned that Michigan parents who invested with his plan, which was offered through another Midwestern state, would forfeit a valuable state tax deduction. Michigan only awards a tax break for educational contributions that residents make to its own state plan.

What's more, the sales rep never once mentioned how much the 529 plan would cost (gouge) the parents. I knew that the plan was outrageously expensive, but I doubt anybody else in the room appreciated that except the guy at the podium. I looked at the handouts to see whether costs were mentioned, but naturally they weren't.

If you ever cross paths with someone who is eager to help you finance a college education, you need to be leery. Although there are many excellent financial planners and Certified Public Accountants who can help you, the niche contains financial pretenders who are primarily interested in lining their own pockets.

In this chapter, you'll learn more on how to differentiate between the posers and the experts.

529 Plan Assistance

If you've ever been approached by someone selling 529 plans, you might have walked away believing that a 529 savings plan is a magic elixir. Listen to the salesman long enough and you might assume that the 529 is the Easter bunny, Santa, and tooth fairy all rolled up in one investment product.

The hyperbole is understandable when you consider that 529 plans are just about all that many investment professionals recommend to families who are freaking out about college costs. Most parents who invest in a 529 plan have heard the sales spiel. In fact, the vast majority of families who invest in 529 plans do so through stockbrokers and other professionals.

The 529 plan can be a wonderful tool, but rarely do families get a glimpse behind the curtain to see how the investment really works—much less how it's marketed.

Here are some of the things you won't hear: The brokers and planners who peddle 529 plans largely depend on commissions for their livelihood. Consequently, the articulate and seemingly sincere salesperson who has gained your trust could be steering you to a mediocre 529 plan saddled with high costs because, hey, he or she can pocket a fat commission.

A study conducted by researchers at the universities of Kansas and Tennessee suggested that salespeople hawking 529 plans are, in fact, steering people to pricey 529 versions. The study revealed that the 529 plans with high fees are more popular than the state plans that offer tax deductions.

The greed factor also explains another common practice. Brokers and others who live off commissions have too often failed to tell clients that they could be forfeiting a state tax break if they choose a 529 outside their own state. That's what I witnessed in Michigan. While a state's plan might not be the best choice, every parent should at least know up front whether their state 529 provides a tax break.

Here's something else that rarely—if ever—gets discussed: The folks peddling 529 plans are often just salespersons. The typical stockbroker is not a financial planner, rather his job is to process financial transactions such as trading stocks or buying municipal bonds for you. If you think the guy providing you with college advice isn't a stockbroker, keep this in mind: Titles are misleading. No one calls themselves stockbrokers anymore. The preferred titles include financial consultant, wealth manager, and adviser.

Whether you should invest in a 529, an educational alternative, or, more likely, a combination of investments isn't something that these salespersons are qualified to discuss. It's simpler for them to take the position that everybody needs a 529. What few parents also realize is that brokers are often wearing blinders. Every state offers 529 plans, but many brokerage firms only permit their brokers to sell one or two plans. Are those going to be the best ones out there? I think you already know that answer.

There's no reason to use a broker or other commissioned person to simply pick a 529 plan. In Chapter 49, "A 529 Primer," you learn about excellent, low-cost plans that you can buy without a middle man.

Financial Planners and Education Advice

The hard part isn't picking a 529. That's easy. The tough part is knowing how to mix and match a 529 plan with the bewildering number of options for parents who want to save for college. In addition to 529 plans, the possibilities include the Coverdell Education Savings Account, Individual Retirement Accounts, custodial accounts, taxable accounts, and that favorite gift for newborns—savings bonds. Once teenagers are ready for college, it's equally challenging to figure out what assets should be tapped to pay for college, which loans are most appropriate, and how the financial aid process works.

Rather than muddle through the process alone, some families may want to seek professional help. If you ultimately decide to look for outside help, first and foremost you should find an advisor who is a *fiduciary*. A fiduciary is someone who must act in good faith when advising his or her clients. A fiduciary must recommend investments that are in the client's best interest. It's only natural to assume that any financial professional should be abiding by those simple guidelines, but they aren't. Only registered investment advisors must, by law, put the interests of their customers first.

In contrast, many stockbrokers do not have to behave as fiduciaries. In fact, their first allegiance is to their brokerage firms. Rather than recommend only the best investments for their clients, they get to observe a lower standard. Their investment recommendations only have to be "suitable." That might not sound bad, but the consequences can kill your wallet. Brokers, for instance, are free to recommend 529 plans that are engorged with fees because even a Porky Pig 529 can be considered "suitable."

Before hiring a financial expert, make sure the advisor will sign in writing that he or she is a fiduciary. Many stockbrokers cannot sign that kind of statement. If you stick with a registered investment advisor, who by law must be a fiduciary, examine his or her ADV-Form, which is filed annually with the U.S. Securities and Exchange Commission. The form, which you should be able to obtain from the advisor, contains such information as the advisor's background, fees, and any regulatory troubles.

One excellent place to look for qualified college experts is the National Institute of Certified College Planners, which provides training and certification for investment professionals. You can hunt for experts who have earned a designation called the Certified College Planning Specialist (CCPS) on the institute's Web site at www.niccp.com.

Since the institute was founded in 2002, hundreds of professionals have been certified. Many of the graduates are Certified Financial Planners and Certified Public Accountants, but the ranks also include stockbrokers and insurance agents. When searching for someone with a CCPS designation, you don't have to confine your search to your own city or state. Many college experts work with families across the country.

Many college planners specialize in helping affluent families who won't qualify for need-based financial aid. Planners steer these families to a variety of legitimate tax write-offs and deductions that can significantly reduce their financial burden. Others work mostly with middle-class families who have a shot at getting financial aid.

When seeking outside advice, watch out for the piranha. Some insurance agents and brokers have dived into this niche as a way to sell life insurance and variable annuities to unsuspecting parents. Life insurance is an expensive and unnecessary way to invest for college, as are variable annuities.

Some of these sharks who are angling for big commissions encourage parents to transfer their home equity into insurance products so the money will escape the notice of financial aid formulas. What these ethically challenged salesmen don't tell people is that the vast majority of schools don't even examine the value of a home. If someone suggests cashing in your home equity for an annuity or life insurance, run.

Action Plan

There are a lot of sharks out there who are only pretending to be college experts. Stick with reputable experts who have impressive financial credentials.

Part XI

The Folks Back Home

53

Parents Behaving Badly

Contrary to what some educators believe, students who frequently talk with their parents and follow their advice participate more frequently in educationally purposeful activities and are more satisfied with their college experience.

—National Survey of Student Engagement

You've probably heard the scathing news accounts about helicopter parents. The media tends to describe them with the same disgust that most of us would reserve for clogged sinks and fender benders.

These are the parents who hover over their kids—constantly. They nag their teenagers to excel, and they grow jealous of the accomplishments of other kids. Forgetting just who is going to college, they commandeer the college admission process. Some college administrators call the worst of the bunch Black Hawk parents.

Although these are the parents who tend to attract negative publicity, I believe their numbers have been greatly exaggerated. I suspect there are far more moms and dads who aren't hovering. In fact, they have checked out. They don't express much interest in where the kids go to college. They figure their child will probably enroll at the nearest community college or state university. Those might indeed be ideal choices for their kids, but there could be better alternatives that they'd discover if they spent just a little time focusing on their children's' education.

Both types of parents are extremes. Your task, of course, is to draw a line between these outliers and find a comfortable middle. And here's why: You can't expect 17- and 18-year-olds to navigate the college journey on their own. It's just not realistic. If you let them experience this adventure by themselves, they might have to settle for an inappropriate choice. They could also easily miss deadlines for financial aid or something else that's important.

If you're the parent of a teenager who is trying to make sense of the whole college admission experience, here is what you should do:

Remind yourself of who's heading to college. Too many parents who become consumed by the college process, secretly or not so secretly believe that their kid will be an academic dud if he doesn't win admission into a school that makes others jealous. You should not measure your own self worth by the school your child ultimately attends or the ones that turn her down. The goal shouldn't be to gather a fistful of acceptance letters that will wow your snootiest friends, but to find schools that fit a child academically, socially, and emotionally. Focus on what's best for your child. Your friends aren't the ones paying the bill nor will they suffer the consequences of a college match gone awry.

Don't assume your alma mater is the best choice. I know a wonderful girl whose parents convinced her that she needed to attend a particular Ivy League school. The university remained the girl's No. 1 choice even though her grades—while respectable—weren't going to win her an acceptance. Why the unrealistic push? The mother was an alum.

In pursuing the family's Ivy League fantasies, the girl enrolled at a state school a few miles away. She hopes to earn great grades there and ultimately transfer. Although the girl might end up being happy at the state school or the Ivy League school, if she manages to transfer, she never appeared to enjoy the freedom to explore other schools. Of course, this mom is hardly the first parent—or the last—to want her child to attend her alma mater. But every child needs his or her own college experience.

Don't rely on hunches. Kids aren't the only ones who fall in love with a school, so do parents. And this is a great way to short circuit an honest examination of the qualities that individual schools possess. I talked with a mom, for instance, who believed that a prestigious school in Southern California represented some sort of educational nirvana for her daughter. The daughter is a phenomenal singer and wants to major in voice. Because the mom was so excited about the school, I assumed that she had already determined that the university offered this major. The reason she thought this would be the perfect fit was because of its small size and gorgeous location. But that wasn't all. She had met people who had attended the school and had seen a car drive by with the school's bumper sticker on it. Ultimately, she had a strong hunch that this was the right school. As it turned out, the school didn't even offer her daughter's intended major.

Ask your child what he or she needs. The time to ask your son or daughter how you can be helpful should come long before the deadlines for college applications are looming. Often, the most helpful thing you can do, before or after your child starts college is to listen. Just listening and empathizing with your child can be difficult. If your child is questioning whether she wants to continue pursuing a degree in art history or philosophy, telling her that accounting or computer science majors make a ton more money isn't going to be helpful.

Have a money talk. Unfortunately, many parents string their kids along during the entire college hunt. Plenty of parents never set parameters on how much money they can afford to spend on college, so the kids assume that they can aim for the academic stars. When a child gets accepted into expensive schools, the parents have to share the bad news that they can't afford them. Now that's just cruel.

Don't get hung up on the wrong things. If you want a welcome antidote to the commercialization of college admissions, read a slim book, *College Unranked, Ending the College Admission Frenzy*. Lloyd Thacker, the executive director of The Education Conservancy (www.educationconservancy.org), wrote the book, which was published by Harvard University Press. Thacker, who spent 30 years in the college admissions field, left the profession to create a movement to decommercialize the college admissions process. Thacker is the force behind the decision of dozens of college and university presidents to refuse to provide information that *U.S. News & World Report* relies on to rank institutions. The book includes many essays, mostly from college administrators who passionately convey what they think is important when looking for colleges. They firmly believe that a student's skills and attitude about learning are far more important than what school he or she attends.

Parent Checklist

The Education Conservancy developed this handy list of guidelines for parents:

- Recognize that gaining admission to college is merely one step in a process of education that will include your student attending a college where she or he can maximize talents and growth. Emphasize the education.
- Resist doing for your students what they are capable of doing for themselves.
- Allow your child to take responsibility for his or her own part of the college application process. Be involved in the process, but do not try to control it.
- Resist relying on rankings and college selectivity to determine the most suitable colleges for your child.
- Realize that researching, selecting, and applying to colleges does not have to be an expensive process.
- Resist attempts to turn the process into a status competition. Develop a healthy, educationally based, and family-appropriate approach to college admissions.
- Consider that gaming the system may not only diminish your child's self-confidence, it may also jeopardize desired admission outcomes.
- Listen to, encourage, and believe in your child. Do not use the term "we" as in "we are applying to...."
- Discuss the idea of education as an ongoing process, and how selecting a college might be different from buying a product.
- Love them enough to let them demonstrate the independence you have instilled in them.
- Keep this process in perspective. Remember that student skills, self-confidence, curiosity, and desire to learn are some of the most important ingredients in a quality education and successful college admissions. Do not sacrifice these by overemphasizing getting into the "best" college.

Keep the process manageable. The more colleges your child applies to, the more expensive and complicated the process will be. It could easily cost you $50 or more for every application your child completes, but even if money isn't an issue, the sheer amount of work required for every application can be daunting. Beginning in the fall of a child's senior year, the onslaught of deadlines can overwhelm even a kid with great organizational skills.

Remain optimistic and supportive. You may wish that your daughter had more meaningful extracurricular activities or that her grade point average was 3.8 instead of 3.1. You may think she botched the interview at her dream school or that your son's guidance counselor is a loser. But you know what? You've got to keep your negative thoughts to yourself. The college process is stressful enough for your child without making it worse.

Don't try to fix everything. Once college moving day has come and gone, resist the temptation to interfere. Admittedly, it's going to be awfully tempting to get on the phone to the housing office if your child hates his roommate, who enjoys watching TV until 3 a.m. It will be just as hard to resist if your child believes his organic chemistry professor is a vindictive tyrant hell-bent on making sure he never gets into medical school.

Why should kids resolve their own problems? For starters, if you continue to run interference for your child, it may never stop. For some parents, it apparently doesn't.

That doesn't mean, however, that you should cut your ties. A generation or two ago, parents might have tried to reach a student once a week on the communal dorm phone down the hall. With cell phones, however, parents and their children are used to talking far more frequently. And studies suggest that many students want that connection.

In a recent survey by UCLA's Higher Education Research Institute, a quarter of freshmen said their parents had "too little" involvement in selecting their college courses and activities. In another study, the National Survey of Student Engagement suggested that students, who had frequent contact with their parents, studied more, interacted with faculty and their peers in a more meaningful way, and generally were more satisfied with college life.

Action Plan

If you follow the Education Conservancy's parental checklist, you will be doing your child a great favor.

54

Getting Grandma to Help

Nobody can do for little children what grandparents do. Grandparents sort of sprinkle stardust over the lives of little children.

—Alex Haley, actor

With college costs defying any and all gravitational pulls, plenty of financially able grandparents are helping with the bills. While generous grandparents should be applauded, sometimes their largess can backfire. If they want to help, they need to understand the right ways to do just that.

Here's what grandparents need to know before they write any checks:

Reevaluate paying the tab directly. Some grandparents assume that the best way to help their grandkids is to send a check directly to the college. But here's where the generosity can backfire: Many universities will shrink the size of a child's financial aid package by the amount of the grandparent's check. If a school has awarded the student $15,000 and grandma mailed the university a check for $15,000, the financial aid could vanish.

Before writing a check, a grandparent should contact the school and ask whether the payment would jeopardize the child's financial aid award. This obviously won't be an issue if the school is not providing any financial assistance to the child.

Wait awhile. If a direct tuition payment would hurt a grandchild's financial aid prospects, other alternatives exist. Grandparents could give the money to the child after his or her last financial aid forms are submitted in the spring of his or her junior year in college. Yet another option is to give the cash to the parents, who unlike their child, would not be required to mention the gift on the Free Application for Federal Student Aid (FAFSA), which is the federal financial aid document that any family hoping to receive federal assistance must fill out.

Evaluate a custodial account. These accounts are a bad idea if a grandchild will eventually qualify for financial aid. The common custodial accounts are the Uniform Transfers to Minors Act (UTMA) and the Uniform Gifts to Minors Act (UGMA), which grandparents can open at many financial institutions.

Financial aid formulas penalize families who save through these accounts. The formulas assume that money in a student's name can be used to pay for tuition. A Harvard University professor once estimated that every dollar sunk into one of these accounts would reduce financial aid by $1.24 over four years. Once again, however, keeping your distance from custodial accounts is only necessary if your child or grandchild might be eligible for need-based aid.

What if a family member has already stashed money in a custodial account? One possibility is escorting the cash into a custodial 529 plan. States offer custodial 529s just like the regular 529 accounts, and they contain the same investment options. Custodial money must be put in custodial 529s because the cash technically belongs to the child.

Traditionally, custodial 529 plans, but not the regular 529 accounts, triggered the same onerous financial aid penalties as custodial accounts. Congress, however, thankfully got rid of this double standard. Starting July 1, 2009, custodial 529 plans will be treated more favorably as a parent asset if the student is a dependent. Up until then, FAFSA won't even ask about custodial 529 plans if the child is a dependent.

Consider a 529 plan. For grandparents, 529 plans offer a tantalizing bonus. State governments created their own 529 plans to help families save for college without getting pelted by taxes. All the money that you sink into one of these tax cocoons can typically be withdrawn for college without triggering taxes. What's more, about half the states provide some sort of tax deduction for contributions to their own plans.

In theory, 529 plans sound great, but too many of these programs are riddled with mediocre investment choices that erode returns with outlandish fees. These plans can only be a prudent way to save for college if you remain selective.

The 529 plan does offer a particularly great deal to grandparents. The federal financial aid formula overlooks any money that grandparents sink into a 529 plan. This isn't the case with 529 accounts that parents open because the federal formula looks at assets that the child and parents own. Consequently, when grandparents save through a 529, their grandkids might have a better shot of qualifying for financial aid.

Coordinate your giving. If you're saving money for your kids' college education and so are the grandparents, you need to coordinate your efforts. That's because some college investing choices demand coordinating. The Coverdell Education Savings Account, for instance, has a low annual contribution ceiling that could easily be violated without parents and grandparents talking. Federal rules require that contributions from all sources—parents, grandparents, or anybody else—not exceed more than $2,000 a year.

Investing in a Roth Individual Retirement Account can create a similar problem. Creating a Roth for a child can be a wonderful way to save for college, but you can't contribute more than the student earns. So if a grandchild makes $4,000 working in a mall food court for a year, you couldn't kick in more than $4,000 in the Roth. And this assumes that the child or the parents don't sock money away in a Roth. The contribution from all the sources couldn't exceed the grandchild's yearly paycheck.

Action Plan

Grandparents can be a godsend when helping with college costs, but make sure they don't sabotage their grandchildren's chances for financial aid.

Appendix: The College Solution Cheat Sheet

If you've read up to this page, you've got a lot to digest. To make the job easier, you'll find many of the key points here that were scattered throughout the book.

Capturing Financial Aid

1. If you educate yourself on your financial and academic choices, you are far more likely to slash the cost of college.
2. Use an online financial aid calculator to help determine whether you will ultimately receive financial aid. The verdict should influence what colleges you look at.
3. If you qualify for financial aid, look for generous schools that provide mostly need-based grants rather than loans in their aid packages.
4. You're more likely to capture an attractive financial aid package if you look for schools that represent a great academic fit.
5. Boost your chances of financial aid by starting to plan well in advance of your child's high school graduation.
6. Even if you're wealthy, always apply for financial aid.
7. Double-check financial aid applications for mistakes. Try negotiating if you receive a disappointing aid package.

Capturing Tuition Discounts

1. Never assume that you must pay full price for a college education.
2. If you won't qualify for need-based aid, focus on schools that offer merit scholarships, which are commonly referred to as tuition discounts.
3. Many colleges and universities offer tuition discounts, and "B" students can qualify for this money at many schools.
4. Measure a school's generosity by examining its Common Data Set numbers.
5. Create demand for your child to boost his or her chances of capturing merit aid.
6. When appropriate, play the gender card to increase your chances of admission and merit money.

Finding Great Academic Fits

1. Don't rely on any book as the ultimate source of information on a particular college. Do your own research.
2. Don't put much weight on *U.S. News & World Report*'s college rankings because the magazine's methodology is greatly flawed.
3. Consider looking beyond brand names to find incredible schools.
4. When exploring schools, use the list of questions that the National Survey for Student Engagement developed.
5. Take advantage of free Internet tools to research colleges easily.
6. Research potential academic majors before shopping for colleges.
7. Never assume that an academic department is great just because the school's overall reputation is sterling.

8. Use press coverage, a department's own Web site, and easy-to-access online resources when evaluating an academic discipline within a school.
9. Look for schools that provide research opportunities to undergraduates.

Overlooked Academic Choices

1. Stay calm. The vast majority of students get accepted by their No. 1 academic choice.
2. When exploring your options, don't overlook private and public liberal arts colleges, which offer a more intimate learning environment.
3. If you expect to attend a large university, look for institutions that strive to make sure that their undergraduates, and especially freshmen, don't get lost in the shuffle.

Exploring Community Colleges

1. A community college can be an excellent way to begin your college experience.
2. A community college provides smaller classes and a less expensive learning experience for freshmen and sophomores.
3. When looking at schools, refer to the questions that the Community College Survey of Student Engagement formulated.
4. Make sure that your hard-earned credits will eventually transfer to a four-year institution.

College Admission Nuts and Bolts

1. If you perform poorly on the SAT, consider applying to schools where the test isn't required.
2. Don't write your college essay like it's an English term paper. Avoid using stilted language and write from your heart.
3. To get the most out of your visits, plan ahead and don't rush through the time spent on campuses.
4. Research a school before an interview and be prepared to ask intelligent questions.
5. Students who overlook all the deadlines or only receive rejection letters should check the Web site of the National Association for College Admission Counseling (www.nacacnet.org) in the spring for schools with vacancies.
6. It's easier to stay organized by following a college timeline.
7. Get the most out of your own high school counselor, who can be a valuable resource.
8. Private college counselors can be invaluable, but make sure your interests mesh with the counselor's objectives.

College Diversity

1. Despite significant challenges, there are many opportunities for enterprising minority students who know where to look for a great education.

Economizing for College

1. Look for schools that have high four-year graduation rates, and you'll save yourself a ton of money.
2. Check for bargains in nearby states.

3. Students should pay for a portion of their college costs. Having a part-time job can actually improve a student's grades.
4. Check out schools that don't charge tuition.
5. Unless a student is a stellar standout, focus on regional or local private scholarships. These outside scholarships are rarely as lucrative as merit awards that schools distribute.

Navigating the Student Loan Maze

1. Don't assume that colleges will recommend the best lenders; look beyond a school's lender list.
2. Select federal loans first and avoid private loans.
3. Always ask whether a loan comes with a discount and look for up-front discounts, which are superior to those imposing waiting periods.
4. Do whatever you can to avoid defaulting on a student loan.

Maximizing College Accounts

1. Avoid expensive 529 plans and stick with low-cost plans that you can buy directly.
2. If you're not sure how to divide your college accounts among investments, consider using the model portfolios that major mutual fund companies rely on.
3. You may unleash unnecessary taxes if you don't know the college account withdrawal rules.

The Folks Back Home

1. Beware of sharks who are only pretending to be college experts.
2. Do your child a great favor and follow the Education Conservancy's parent checklist.

3. Grandparents can be a godsend when helping with college costs, but make sure they don't sabotage their grandchildren's chances for financial aid.

Resource Guide

Academic Accreditation Agencies

Council for Higher Education Accreditation, www.chea.org/directories/special.asp

U.S. Department of Education's database of accredited postsecondary institutions and programs, http://ope.ed.gov/accreditation/

Academic Quality

College Navigator, Institute of Education Sciences, National Center for Education Statistics, www.nces.ed.gov/collegenavigator

Community College Survey of Student Engagement, www.ccsse.org

The Education Conservancy, www.educationconservancy.org

National Survey of Student Engagement, www.nsse.iub.edu

Center of Inquiry in the Liberal Arts at Wabash College, www.liberalarts.wabash.edu/cila

The Teagle Foundation, www.teaglefoundation.org

Canadian Schools

Association of Universities and Colleges of Canada, www.aucc.ca

SchoolFinder.com, www.schoolfinder.com

College Advisors

Higher Education Consultants Association, www.hecaonline.org

Independent Educational Consultants Association, www.educationalconsulting.org

National Institute of Certified College Planners, www.niccp.com

College Applications

Common Application, www.commonapp.org

Community Colleges

Community College Survey of Student Engagement, www.ccsse.org

Jack Kent Cooke Foundation, www.jackkentcookefoundation.org

Phi Theta Kappa, www.ptk.org

Financial Aid

Economic Diversity of Colleges, www.economicdiversity.org

FinAid, www.finaid.org

FinancialAidLetter.com, www.financialaidletter.com

U.S. Department of Education, Federal Student Aid, www.studentaid.ed.gov

Financial Aid Applications

CSS/Financial Aid PROFILE, https://profileonline.collegeboard.com

Free Application for Federal Student Aid (FAFSA), www.fafsa.ed.gov

529 Plans

Independent 529 Plan, www.independent529plan.org

Morningstar, www.morningstar.com

SavingForCollege.com, www.savingforcollege.com

Graduation Rates

College Navigator, Institute of Education Sciences, National Center for Education Statistics, www.nces.ed.gov/collegenavigator

The Education Trust's College Results Online, www.collegeresults.org

Higher Education Press Coverage & Trends

The Chronicle of Higher Education, http://chronicle.com

Inside Higher Ed, www.insidehighered.com

The Journal of Blacks in Higher Education**,** www.jbhe.com

New America Foundation's Higher Ed Watch blog, www.newamerica.net/blog/higher_ed_watch

College Board's Trends in Higher Education, http://professionals.collegeboard.com/data-reports-research/trends

Interviews

A Pocket Guide to Choosing a College: Are You Asking the Right Questions?, http://nsse.iub.edu/html/students_parents.cfm

Learning Communities

Residential Learning Communities International Clearinghouse, Bowling Green State University, http://pcc.bgsu.edu/rlcch/

Washington Center for Improving the Quality of Undergraduate Education www.evergreen.edu/washcenter/project.asp?pid=73

Minorities and Colleges

Black Excel, www.blackexcel.org

Bureau of Indian Education, U.S. Department of the Interior, www.oiep.bia.edu

The Congressional Hispanic Caucus Institute, www.chci.org

Economic Diversity of Colleges, www.economicdiversity.org/

The HBCU (Historically Black Colleges and Universities) Network, www.hbcunetwork.com

Hispanic Association of Colleges & Universities, www.hacu.net

Hispanic Scholarship Fund, www.hsf.net

The Journal of Blacks in Higher Education, www.jbhe.com

National Association of Hispanic Publications Foundation's Scholarships for Hispanics, www.scholarshipsforhispanics.org

Tribal College Journal of American Indian Higher Education, www.tribalcollegejournal.org

Private Colleges and Universities

Council of Independent Colleges, www.cic.edu/makingthecase/index.asp

National Association of Independent Colleges and Universities, www.naicu.edu

University and College Accountability Network (U-CAN), www.ucan-network.org

Researching Schools

AdmissionsAdvice.com, www.admissionsadvice.com

College Confidential, www.collegeconfidential.com

College Navigator, Institute of Education Sciences, National Center of Education Statistics, www.nces.ed.gov/collegenavigator

Common Data Set, To find each school's "Common Data Set," type the term into the institution's online search engine.

The Education Trust's College Results Online, www.collegeresults.org

University and College Accountability Network (U-CAN), www.ucan-network.org

SAT/ACT Preparation

ACT, www.act.org

National Center for Fair and Open Testing (FairTest), www.fairtest.org

Number2.com, www.number2.com

SAT (College Board), http://www.collegeboard.com/student/testing/sat/prep_one/prep_one.html

Scholarships

College Board's Scholarship Search,
http://apps.collegeboard.com/cbsearch_ss/welcome.jsp

FastWeb!, www.fastweb.com

Federal Trade Commission, www.ftc.gov/scholarshipscams
(877) FTC-HELP

Scholarships.com, www.scholarhips.com

Student Loans

Credit Bureaus:

Equifax, (800) 685-1111, www.equifax.com

Experian, (888) 397-3742, www.experian.com

TransUnion, (800) 888-4213, www.transunion.com

FinAid, www.finaid.org

National Consumer Law Center's Student Loan Borrower Assistance Project,
www.studentloanborrowerassistance.org

Project on Student Debt, www.projectonstudentdebt.org

StudentLoanJustice.org, www.studentloanjustice.org

Teacher Evaluations

Pick-A-Prof, www.pickaprof.com

ProfessorPerformance.com,
www.professorperformance.com

RateMyProfessors.com, www.ratemyprofessors.com

Text Books

Amazon.com, www.amazon.com
Barnes & Noble, www.barnesandnoble.com
Best Book Buys, www.bestbookbuys.com

Undergraduate Research

Council on Undergraduate Research, www.cur.org
Web Guide to Research for Undergraduates (WebGURU), www.webguru.neu.edu

Working Colleges

Work Colleges Consortium, www.workcolleges.org

INDEX

A

D

E

F

J

K

L

R

S

T

U

V

W

X–Z